SPIRITUAL
Lightening

M. CATHERINE THOMAS

DESERET
BOOK

SALT LAKE CITY, UTAH

Visit us at deseretbook.com

First printing in hardbound 1996
First printing in paperbound 1998

Library of Congress Catalog Card Number: 96-83938

ISBN 0-88494-982-6 (hardbound)
ISBN-10 1-57008-518-8 (paperbound)
ISBN-13 978-1-57008-518-5 (paperbound)

Printed in the United States of America
R. R. Donnelley

20 19

To my children, Laura, Jennifer, Christopher, Amy, Jefferson, and Anne, who have taught me with patience and forgiveness and who have filled their own lives with goodness. And to my husband, Gordon, with whom so many wonderful things have been possible.

Contents

Contents

CHAPTER ONE

The Veil of Unbelief

"Come unto me, O ye Gentiles," the Lord has said, "and I will show unto you the greater things, the knowledge which is hid up because of unbelief. . . . Behold, when ye shall rend that veil of unbelief. . . ." (Ether 4:13, 15.)

The answers to our problems often lie just beyond the veils of our unbelief, as was the case when Ammon was teaching Lamoni the plan of redemption. When Ammon had finished, the Lamanite king cried out in prayer and fell to the earth as if dead. But Ammon, undismayed, knew "that king Lamoni was under the power of God; he knew that the *dark veil of unbelief* was being cast away from his mind, and the light which did light up his mind, which was the light of the glory of God, which was a marvelous light of his goodness—yea, this light had infused such joy into his soul, the cloud of darkness having been dispelled, and that the light of everlasting life was lit up in his soul, yea, he knew that . . . he was carried away in God" (Alma 19:6).

When the dark veil of unbelief was cast away from Lamoni's mind, he was infused with spiritual light and joy. The king's experience serves as a pattern for each Latter-day Saint. It need not be so dramatic and compressed as Lamoni's to be very potent. Here is a more gradual description of the process: "And now, my brethren, I desire that ye shall plant this word [the doctrine of Christ] in your hearts, and as it beginneth to swell even so nourish it by your faith. And behold, it will become a tree, springing up in you unto everlasting life. And then may God grant unto you that your burdens may be light, through the joy of his Son. And even all this can ye do if ye will." (Alma 33:23.)

Having burdens lightened through the joy of the Lord Jesus Christ requires planting in the soul a spiritual knowledge of things as they really are (see Jacob 4:13). Much of the heaviness that we bear develops from a faith that is not sufficiently informed. The danger of having an undernourished faith is that one is vulnerable to false ideas that darken the veil and increase one's burdens.

Nephi, looking down the ages, saw the dangers the Saints would face in the latter days and put us on alert: "There shall be many which shall teach . . . false and vain and foolish doctrines, and shall be puffed up in their hearts. . . . They have all gone astray save it be a few, who are the humble followers of Christ; nevertheless, they are led, that in many instances they do err because they are taught by the precepts of men. . . . Yea, wo be unto him that hearkeneth unto the precepts of men, and denieth the power of God, and the gift of the Holy Ghost! . . . Cursed is he that putteth his trust in man, or maketh flesh his arm, or shall hearken unto the precepts of men, save their precepts shall be given by the power of the Holy Ghost." (2 Nephi 28:9, 14, 26, 31.)

The sobering message in these verses is that not only people in general but also many Saints would be led by the precepts of men. This prophetic insight offers a compassionate warning and a call to receive greater lightening. If relatively few of the Saints have discerned these precepts of men, these errors are probably rather subtle and hard to detect. But scripture describes them, and the prophets point them out. President Ezra

Taft Benson taught: "God, with his infinite foreknowledge, so molded the Book of Mormon that we might see the error and know how to combat false educational, political, religious, and philosophical concepts of our time" ("The Book of Mormon Is the Word of God," *Ensign*, May 1975, p. 64).

The real problem with false ideas, as Nephi reveals (see 2 Nephi 28:5), is that they influence many to deny the power of God and therefore to deprive themselves of the power of God in their lives. The precepts of men partake of the philosophy of Korihor the anti-Christ, who taught that man prospered only by his own genius and strength and not by God's power (see Alma 30:17). It is not so much that we have denied the existence of the power of God as that we have denied ourselves of that power by implementing false ideas. The Lord warns of that latter-day "spirit which hath so strongly riveted the creeds of the fathers, who have inherited lies, upon the hearts of the children" (D&C 123:7). To some greater or lesser extent, each of us is one of those children.

Not by deliberate consent, but mostly inadvertently, we all have the precepts of men riveted on our hearts just by virtue of being born into a fallen world. We have absorbed them without question through growing up and living in a fallen world. It is part of the heritage of the natural man. And we may have embraced additional false ideas because of our ignorance of God's revealed laws—"My people are gone into captivity, because they have no knowledge" (2 Nephi 15:13). The Lord, knowing our dilemma better than we do, compassionately warns: "Beware concerning yourselves, to give diligent heed to the words of eternal life. For you shall live by every word that proceedeth forth from the mouth of God" (D&C 84:43–44).

But we may need to learn more of what the Lord has actually said in order to be able to live by it. He continues:

Your minds in times past have been darkened because of unbelief, and because you have treated lightly the things you have received—

Which vanity and unbelief have brought the whole church under condemnation.

And this condemnation resteth upon the children of Zion, even all.

And they shall remain under this condemnation until they repent and remember the new covenant, even the Book of Mormon and the former commandments which I have given them, not only to say, but to do according to that which I have written—

That they may bring forth fruit meet for their Father's kingdom; otherwise there remaineth a scourge and judgment to be poured out upon the children of Zion. (D&C 84:54–58.)

President Ezra Taft Benson instructed the Latter-day Saints in general conference:

It is important that in our teaching we make use of the *language* of holy writ. Alma said, "I . . . do command you in the language of him who hath commanded me" (Alma 5:61).

The words and the way they are used in the Book of Mormon by the Lord should become our source of understanding and should be used by us in teaching gospel principles. . . .

We need to use the everlasting word to awaken those in deep sleep so they will awake "unto God."

I am deeply concerned about what we are doing to teach the Saints at all levels the gospel of Jesus Christ as completely and authoritatively as do the Book of Mormon and the Doctrine and Covenants. By this I mean teaching the "great plan of the Eternal God," to use the words of Amulek (Alma 34:9). ("The Book of Mormon and the Doctrine and Covenants," *Ensign*, May 1987, p. 84; emphasis added.)

According to President Benson, all of our teachings should be circumscribed by the "great plan of the Eternal God." Elder Dallin H. Oaks adds a yet finer point on what our precepts should include: "The reality of our total dependence upon Jesus Christ for the attainment of our goals of immortality and eternal life should dominate every teaching and every testimony and every action of every soul touched by the light of the restored gospel. If we teach every other subject and principle with perfection and fall short on this one, we have failed in our most important mission." (Sins, Crimes and Atonement, CES, "An Evening with Elder Dallin H. Oaks," 7 February 1992, p. 3.)

The world cannot help but study the human being outside of this eternal plan of God, thus distorting the truth about how human beings flourish in the fullest sense. These truncated teachings about the nature of man become the precepts of men because, cut off from the eternal plan of God, they necessarily deny the power of God. Man's spiritual, emotional, even physical well-being cannot be studied meaningfully outside the plan of the Eternal God.

The most dangerous precepts of men may have the form of godliness; that is, they may sound high principled, but, as the Lord said to Joseph Smith, they deny the power of godliness (see Joseph Smith—History 1:19). The Savior said to his Apostles about our day, "For in those days there shall also arise false Christs, and false prophets, and shall show great signs and wonders, insomuch, that, if possible, they shall deceive the very elect, who are the elect according to the covenant. . . . And whoso treasureth up my word, shall not be deceived." (Joseph Smith—Matthew 1:22, 37.) Speaking of the Joseph Smith Translation of the Bible, the Lord said, in fact, that the scriptures would be given "to the salvation of mine own elect" (D&C 35:20).

The danger of riveting false concepts upon our hearts, of embracing the precepts and uninspired philosophies of men, is that they limit our perception of the truth and thus inhibit our spiritual power and happiness; they thicken the veil. It does matter what we believe. It does matter what vocabulary we use to describe the nature of man and the means by which he prospers, because so much of the trouble and suffering in our lives rises out of our false assumptions. When we govern our thoughts and our actions by untruth, we reap unhappiness and confusion in the emotional, spiritual, and even physical dimensions of our lives. The assumptions we make about the purpose of the world, God's interaction with his children, and the nature of the people around us and what our relationship should be to them—these make all the difference in the quality of our lives, here and hereafter.

Jeremiah prophesied of our day, implying the solution to our problems: "This shall be the covenant that I will make with the house of Israel . . . I will put my law in their inward parts, and write it in their hearts; and will be their God, and they shall be my people. And they shall teach no more every man his neighbor, and every man his brother, saying, Know the Lord: for they shall all know me, from the least of them unto the greatest of them" (Jeremiah 31:33–34). We must know the word so well that, written in our minds and in our hearts, it becomes the governing force in our lives. In this manner we ignite the power of the Spirit in our inward parts and transcend much of the sorrow of this world.

Having tuned our daily minds to the spirit of prophecy and revelation, we can obtain what is promised in these verses: "If thou shalt ask, thou shalt receive revelation upon revelation, knowledge upon knowledge, that thou mayest know the mysteries and peaceable things—that which bringeth joy, that which bringeth life eternal" (D&C 42:61).

Men's precepts are a burden to the Saints. To embrace the Lord's constructs about how man flourishes is to receive spiritual lightening.

❧

CHAPTER TWO

Spiritual Lightening

When we are weighed down by the sorrows of a telestial world, we need some spiritual lightening. Spiritual lightening suggests spiritual principles and powers that can light up our minds and lighten our loads. It may be that it is possible to assume too great a burden, to take it all too seriously. This is possible even when the damages in our lives involve sex, drugs, and other heavy sorrows—because virtually all damage, innocently incurred or self-inflicted, is ultimately reversible through the Lord Jesus Christ. It is spiritually lightening to realize that in most cases the actual details of the elements of our lives matter less than what we choose to become in the midst of them.

It helps to remember that we came down to a fallen world to experience deliverance from it. The crisis that grips us emotionally may carry a significant message for us. It may be a call from the eternal world to learn something we need to know. Events have a way of conspiring to draw our distracted minds to the voice of the Good Shepherd (see Alma 5:37–38), who may whisper through our distress a truth that we have resisted but must now humbly face. "For behold, the Lord hath said: I will not succor my people in the day of their transgression; but I will hedge up their ways that they prosper not; and their doings shall be as a stumbling block before them. . . . But if ye will turn to the Lord with full purpose of heart, and put your trust in him, and serve him with all diligence of mind, if ye do this, he will, according to his own will and pleasure, deliver you out of bondage." (Mosiah 7:29, 33.)

This higher perspective teaches that we came down to earth to learn from our own experience the difference between good and evil. To make that judgment we had to come to know— that is, experience—some degree of evil.

The experience with truth that we gain here serves as a small-scale pattern for those very same principles that will be used on a grand scale in eternity—the temporal in the likeness of the spiritual (see Moses 6:63; Matthew 25:23). "Whatever principle of intelligence we attain unto in this life, it will rise with us in the resurrection. And if a person gains more knowledge and intelligence in this life through his diligence and obedience than another, he will have so much the advantage in the world to come." (D&C 130:18–19.)

The acquiring of spiritual intelligence through experience in a fallen world is the treasure we've come for. Our most valuable gains in intelligence come from embracing the word of God until we can live by his every word (see D&C 84:44). Thus the natural gives way to the spiritual, and the intelligence we so obtain will endure forever.

It is also helpful to realize that much of what happens here in the temporal world will pass away into the black hole of eternity and find extinction there: damage we suffered from others will be healed, damage we inflicted on others will be mended, ignorance will give way to the full picture, tears will dry, shattered dreams will find new and eternal expression, lessons we thought we learned too late will find application here and in the world to come. Perhaps this good news is what the Lord is telling an anguishing Joseph Smith when He says: "Know thou, my son, that all these things shall give thee experience, and shall be for thy good. . . . Therefore, hold on thy way . . . fear not what man can do, for God shall be with you forever and ever." (D&C 122:7, 9.)

President Joseph F. Smith taught that in the premortal life we knew much of what lay before us:

Can we know anything here that we did not know before we came? . . . I believe that our Savior is the ever-living example to all flesh in all these things. He no doubt possessed a foreknowledge of all the vicissitudes through which he would have to pass in the mortal tabernacle, when the foundations of this earth were laid, "when the morning stars sang together, and all the sons of God shouted for joy." . . . And yet, to accomplish the ultimatum of his previous existence, and consummate the grand and glorious object of his being, and the salvation of his infinite brotherhood, he had to come and take upon him flesh. He is our example. . . . If Christ knew beforehand, so did we. But in coming here, we forgot all, that our agency might be free indeed, to choose good or evil. (Joseph F. Smith, *Gospel Doctrine* [Salt Lake City: Deseret Book, 1977], p. 13.)

So we came to earth to acquire an essential knowledge that was not fully available to us in the premortal world. We had to come and gain the actual experience of making our way through a plan that was designed to bring across our life paths those experiences we most needed to fulfill the purposes of our mortal probation.

God knew that we would arrive in a fallen world with no memory, no knowledge, and no power to make our way successfully alone. Once in mortality, we would begin to make choices before we had much knowledge, or judgment, or ability to choose right over wrong consistently, and we would inevitably make mistakes. As we grew in a fallen environment we would form wrong opinions, make false assumptions by which we would then govern our lives, embrace many precepts of men. We would create a veil of unbelief (see Ether 4:15) and would, as a result, leave a lot of imperfect products behind us. We would make many choices before we had grasped the significance of even the light that we had. Many would reach an advanced age before they really saw the light. Some would never see it in this life. Provision was made according to the circumstances and true desires of all these people.

So we realize that even though the natural man is wonderfully designed to give way to the spiritual (see Mosiah 3:19), he must first, by divine design, experience the errors of the natural mind which would cause him to taste the bitter (2 Nephi 2:15; Moses 6:55). We ourselves may have grown comfortable in the natural mind and may have been slow to give it up. Like Amulek, we might have said: "I did harden my heart, for I was called many times and I would not hear; therefore I knew concerning these things, yet I would not know" (Alma 10:6).

But all the while, life was happening to us; we were making important choices and these were affecting ourselves and others. Our slowness in changing our minds from natural to spiritual may have caused us to create many sorrowful situations.

We came to earth to acquire an essential knowledge that was not fully available to us in the premortal world. Elder Maxwell has written: "Perhaps it helps to emphasize—more than we sometimes do—that our first estate featured learning of a cognitive type, and it was surely a much longer span than that of our second estate, and the tutoring so much better and more direct. The second estate, however, is one that emphasizes *experiential learning* through *applying, proving,* and *testing.* We learn cognitively here too, just as a good university examination also teaches even as it tests us. In any event, the books of the first estate are now closed to us, and the present test is, therefore, very real. We have moved, as it were, from first-estate *theory* to second-estate *laboratory.* It is here that our Christlike characteristics are further shaped and our spiritual skills are thus strengthened." (*All These Things Shall Give Thee Experience* [Salt Lake City: Deseret Book, 1979], pp. 19–20.)

Earth life, then, is something like a laboratory. Our manuals are full of vital instructions, though we may have esteemed them lightly (see D&C 84:54–55) and thus find ourselves in a spiritual twilight. Even when we have understood the purposes of life, there is, at times, an undeniable ambiguity in our lives. We do not always understand our lives because "now we see through a glass, darkly" (1 Corinthians 13:12), and "it doth not yet appear what we shall be" (1 John 3:2). We may grope around in this twilight of knowledge, anxious that someone is going to blow up either our experiment or the whole laboratory altogether. It can seem so out of control.

I may see that some of the people around me in the lab are making some dangerous choices. They're not following instructions, they're using the wrong ingredients. I may see that my husband or my teenage son or my married daughter may not be conducting his or her experiments very wisely.

To my dismay, I find that one of my worst fears is that what they are doing makes *me* look bad. (Didn't I teach them how to do their experiments? Won't the world judge me by the way they are doing their lab work? *Aren't* I responsible for how they are doing their work?) Maybe I think that if I can fix them, and they get fixed, I won't have to feel guilty about them anymore. But here I am trying to fix their lives, no matter that I cannot perfectly conduct my own. How can I keep my hands off their experiments? To what degree am I my brother's experiment keeper? As we harbor feelings of confusion, anger, and fear, the spirit of relief eludes us.

We can see on reflection that one of our greatest stressors may be our own pride, our mixing up our own personal value with what another person is doing. Spiritual lightening helps us to straighten that out, answering one of our hardest questions: Where is the line drawn between my responsibility and his or hers? How do I discern between help and interference? We cleanse our hearts of pride and then can rise above the twilight, oblivious to what our neighbors may think. Soon we can pray: "O Lord, help me to see what appropriate help I can give. Help me to exercise enough faith in thy plan for my loved ones that I can leave them to thee when there is nothing more I can do. Help me then to find a serenity that is independent of what another is doing."

One source of relief lies in scriptural examples illustrating this idea of not letting others' choices ruin one's life and health. Here is Alma, weighed down with sorrow, having been cast out of Ammonihah. An angel appears to him and says: "Blessed art thou, Alma; therefore, lift up thy head and rejoice, for thou hast great cause to rejoice; for thou hast been faithful" (Alma 8:15). A similar idea appears in Ether, where Moroni fears that the Gentiles will not have charity for his words. The Lord responds: "If they have not charity it mattereth not unto thee, *thou* hast been faithful" (Ether 12:37, emphasis added). Obviously the extent of our happiness rests primarily on what we do and not on what another chooses to do. We don't need to let another person's choices hold our happiness prisoner. The Spirit can with its rich feelings of happiness transcend the otherwise unraveling elements of our lives.

But then a little voice says to our fragile hope: "BUT, you *could* have done more; you *shouldn't* have done such and such; you *should* have known; and so forth. You are *not* faithful; *you* caused the problems." That you are even partly to blame for your loved one's trouble may or may not be true. But if I have indeed contributed to a loved one's pain, I can repent. I can make restitution so far as it can be made. After one's heart is truly broken, one might say to another (a mother to a child, or a husband to a wife): "I am so deeply sorry that I caused you damage. Now, given what I know, I would give anything to undo, to re-do, what I did. I wish you could look back on our association together and see me as having done all those things differently. I wish you could recreate the memory and imagine that I acted sensitively, lovingly, patiently, with greater reverence for your agency and your feelings. I now entrust you to the Lord. I will do all for you that I can, but your troubles and your choices are now between you and your Savior."

With respect to discerning what to do for others, here also the Lord is our model. We see that he usually avoids doing for us what we can reasonably do for ourselves—what we need to do for ourselves. Much grace is given *after* or *as* we do all that we can do (see 2 Nephi 25:23). He also often waits for us to ask.

Here, however, are some forms of grace that people greatly need and that can produce unexpected little miracles: empathy, patience, tolerance, forgiveness, listening, kind words, hugs, kisses, smiles, a helping hand, words of encouragement and praise. These are attributes of godliness; they draw the Spirit into our relationships.

We remember as well that very powerful grace which is received through the Holy Ghost for another in the form of inspired words, spiritual gifts, and so forth. Notice that these have little to do with unsolicited advice-giving, or taking over because we think another can't work out his or her own problems with the Lord. We may indeed be called to intervene in another's life quite directly, but this intervention usually comes most effectively after careful spiritual purification, preparation, and planning.

The scriptures teach that the random nature of the laboratory is only apparent. The Lord knows everything that is going to happen in the lab before it does. His perfect foreknowledge doesn't mean that he has chosen everything that is going to happen; rather, it means that he has foreseen what we will choose and has put appropriate measures into place so that his great purposes for the individual lives of his children will not be frustrated. Elder Maxwell has written: "By foreseeing, God can plan and His purposes can be fulfilled, but He does this in a way that does not in the least compromise our individual free agency, any more than an able meteorologist causes the weather rather than forecasts it" (*All These Things Shall Give Thee Experience*, p. 19).

The Lord has put into place appropriate compensations, solutions, and healings—specific to damages that will come and specific to the difficult experiences that each needs. Many of these solutions and compensations will be realized in this life; others, in the world to come. Of course, agency is always operative, and we will often see people not availing themselves of these divine solutions that are presented again and again through the course of life's experiences. Many will choose not to implement them. But those determined to come to the Lord

Jesus Christ will find many, many healings and revelations and opportunities to help them reverse the damages from the mistakes or pain of the past. "The Lord knoweth all things from the beginning; wherefore, he prepareth a way to accomplish all his works among the children of men; for behold, he hath all power unto the fulfilling of all his words" (1 Nephi 9:6).

Elder Boyd K. Packer has said: "Remember that mortal life is a brief moment, for we will live eternally. There will be ample (I almost used the word time, but time does not apply here), there will be ample opportunity for all injustices, all inequities to be made right, all loneliness and deprivation compensated, and all worthiness rewarded when we keep the faith. 'If in this life only we have hope in Christ, we are of all men most miserable' (1 Corinthians 15:19). It does not all end with mortal death; it just begins" ("The Fountain of Life," BYU 18–Stake Fireside, 29 March 1992).

One of my major challenges, then, is to accept and work with those things that happen to me in the laboratory that are for my experience and development and blessing—if I can just turn my thoughts and exercise my faith that way (see 2 Nephi 26:24). The Lord encourages us with these words: "Thou shalt thank the Lord thy God in all things. . . . In nothing doth man offend God, . . . save those who confess not his hand in all things, and obey not his commandments." (D&C 59:7, 21.)

My challenge is to see that each tangled relationship and each stressful situation has a message for me; each is seeking to teach me something I need to know. The message is always pointed toward what it is we are to present at the judgment. Mormon is clear on the product that will be required at the gates of heaven: "Charity is the pure love of Christ, and it endureth forever; and whoso is found possessed of it at the last day, it shall be well with him" (Moroni 7:47). Then Mormon tells how to acquire this gift, illuminating the fact that what we present at heaven's door is the product of our pure desires and the Lord's granting of those desires in the form of spiritual light and godly growth: "Wherefore, my beloved brethren, pray unto the Father with all the energy of heart, that ye may be filled with this love, which he hath bestowed upon all who are true followers of his Son, Jesus Christ; that ye may become the sons of God; that when he shall appear we shall be like him, for we shall see him as he is; that we may have this hope; that we may be purified even as he is pure" (Moroni 7:47–48).

So we realize that a list of perfect works, even if we could produce it, would not suffice alone. But the good news is that if we have repented we don't present a list of bad works at the judgment, either. "And it shall come to pass, that whoso repenteth and is baptized in my name shall be filled; and if he endureth to the end, behold, him will I hold guiltless before my Father at that day when I shall stand to judge the world" (3 Nephi 27:16).

This scripture suggests that repentance, combined with the power in the Atonement, consumes all the imperfect products we've left behind us. The image of the butterfly leaving its lifeless cocoon behind suggests a spiritual metaphor of continuing transformation to greater spiritual beauty. As transformation takes place, the products of the past become biodegradable. I believe the Lord when he says that for the repentant soul no black list is produced from some divine computer at judgment. He promises: "If the wicked will turn from all his sins that he hath committed, and keep all my statutes, and do that which is lawful and right, he shall surely live, he shall not die. All his transgressions that he hath committed, they shall not be mentioned unto him." (Ezekiel 18:21–22.)

I propose that what we finally present at the gates of heaven is the grace we asked for and labored to receive. "Yea, come unto Christ, and be perfected in him, and deny yourselves of all ungodliness; and if ye shall deny yourselves of all ungodliness, and love God with all your might, mind and strength, then is his grace sufficient for you, that by his grace ye may be perfect in Christ; and if by the grace of God ye are perfect in Christ, ye can in nowise deny the power of God" (Moroni 10:32).

The details of our lives may from time to time seem to lie in shambles, but all of this is only apparent and it is only temporary. We are seeking the treasure buried in the shambles. When we move toward the light, Amulek promised, *immediately* the great plan of redemption is brought about unto us (see Alma 34:31). The Lord told Daniel: "Fear not, Daniel: for from the first day that thou didst set thine heart to understand, and to chasten thyself before thy God, thy words were heard" (Daniel 10:12).

When life's burdens get us down, we can ascend in our minds to a higher reality—a truer one. It is possible during troubled times to feel a sweet spiritual lightening steal into our darkened minds with these impressions: "My [child], peace be unto thy soul" (D&C 121:7); "He that keepeth Israel shall neither slumber nor sleep" (Psalm 121:4). It is possible to feel an irrepressible joy even in the midst of seeming chaos, because, as the Apostle Paul teaches, there is a peace which passes understanding (see Philippians 4:7) and a love that passes knowledge (see Ephesians 3:19). In the midst of trouble, one really can just smile and say, like the radio announcer, "This is a test, this is primarily a test, and if I can hang on in loyalty to the Lord and forgive and love and grasp his will, I will have retrieved the hidden treasure here—no matter how things seem to be turning out to the contrary. I will have become acquainted with my Savior, who descended below all things" (see D&C 122:8). We remember the Apostle Paul's testimony:

> I am persuaded, that neither death, nor life, nor angels, nor principalities, nor powers, nor things present, nor things to come, nor height, nor depth, nor any other creature, shall be able to separate us from the love of God, which is in Christ Jesus our Lord (Romans 8:38–39).

CHAPTER THREE

"The Doer of Our Deeds"

A specific precept of man may concern the pursuit of self-esteem. This pursuit spans a wide spectrum of meanings from outright pride-tripping and image manipulation to more spiritually based pursuits; but finally all are designed to enhance one's good feelings about oneself, one's inner comfort and peace.

Each of us has a tender self, and we are quite vulnerable to feeling down on ourselves. As a result of this human condition, there have sprung up many different kinds of books and seminars designed to help people move from low self-esteem to higher levels of self-comfort. These different systems generally prescribe things to do by way of accomplishments, or new ways to think about oneself, or various affirmations to repeat to help one feel better. Many therapists and social scientists have identified low self-esteem as a major source of basic human problems and have suggested that boosting self-esteem helps to solve these problems.

But I would like to suggest that the concept of self-esteem as a solution to man's most basic spiritual, emotional, and even physical needs is not found in the scriptures. One might be surprised to find that in the scriptures there are no positive references to self-esteem, self-confidence, or self-love. Not because God does not feel exquisite tenderness for human beings, but because he knows a better way for human flourishing than focusing on raising self-esteem.

Whatever the valid uses of the term *self-esteem* are, however much good is intended by it, I wonder if self-esteem isn't a red herring. The term *red herring* comes from the practice of dragging this smelly fish across a trail to destroy the original scent. Thus a red herring is a diversion intended to distract attention from the real issue. I suggest that the issue of self-esteem is a diversion to distract us from the real issue of our existence.

We might be justified in telling people to raise their self-esteem in order to solve their most basic problems if we knew nothing of man's premortal life, or the spiritual purpose of his earthly probation, or his glorious destiny. But the fulness of the gospel of Jesus Christ teaches the true nature and true needs of the human self and suggests that one cannot really define man without God.

I suggest that there are two major human conditions that the self is subject to that may have led to the idea that the pursuit of self-esteem was important: 1) man's vulnerability, or even pain, incident to the fall of man; and 2) the conflict or pain created by ignorance of divine law or by personal sin.

First, the pain incident to fallenness. Like our Savior, though to a lesser degree, we condescended to come to a fallen world, having agreed to submit to a considerable reduction in our premortal powers and quality of life. As we came to earth, separated from the presence of heavenly parents, we died spiritually (see Helaman 14:16) and, in a sense, we were "orphaned." And now, with memory veiled, and much reduced from our premortal estate, somewhat as aliens in a world that is inimical to our spiritual natures, we may carry an insecurity, a self-pain, which pervades much of our emotional life. Like Adam and Eve, we feel our self-consciousness or spiritual nakedness. The scriptures teach about this nakedness as a feeling of guilt or shame (e.g., 2 Nephi 9:14; Mormon 9:5). Do we have, as well, a sense of loss from deeply buried memories of who we once were in contrast with who we are now? But here are my main questions: Is it possible that in our efforts to find security we have fallen into a number of errors? Is it possible that we have created the whole issue of self-esteem in an attempt to soothe this fallen, homesick self?

There is a better way to find what our hearts long for than by seeking greater self-esteem. Our Savior, who felt all this pain himself (see Alma 7:11–13), would not send us to earth without compensation for the distresses he knew we would feel, separated from him. He would not leave us comfortless. Recall the passages in John in which the Savior told the Twelve that he would be with them only a little while (John 13:33). Peter responded with "Lord, why cannot I follow thee now? I will lay down my life for thy sake" (vv. 36–37). Jesus, sensing their pain, almost their desperation, at his leaving them, promised, "I will not leave you comfortless: I will come to you" (John 14:18). The English word *comfortless* translates the Greek word for *orphans:* "I will not leave you orphaned." The Savior continues, "If a man love me, he will keep my words: and my Father will love him, and we will come unto him, and make our abode with him" (John 14:23). "My peace I give unto you: not as the world giveth, give I unto you. Let not your heart be troubled, neither let it be afraid." (John 14:27.)

Here we grasp the stunning insight that the Lord Jesus Christ himself is that consolation, that compensation, designed from the foundation of the world to comfort the human pain of fallenness, to compensate men and women for their earthly reductions and sacrifices. Only the Atonement, or more expressly the at-one-ment, of the Redeemer and the redeemed can heal the pain of the Fall. When we feel how much he loves us, we cannot help but love him: "We love him," John writes, "because he first loved us" (1 John 4:19). His love is the consolation.

Now to the second source of pain. The Lord explained, speaking to Adam: "When [thy children] begin to grow up, sin conceiveth in their hearts, and they taste the bitter" (Moses 6:55). What is this bitterness? The Lord says it is the conception of sin in our hearts. The pain of fallenness, then, is compounded by the bitterness of sin.

To understand why sin produces this bitterness, we remember that each individual spirit was begotten by glorious heavenly parents and thereby inherits a nature which, at its very core, is light, truth, intelligence, and glory (see D&C 93:23, 29, 36). "Knowest thou not," the prophet John Taylor wrote, "that thou art a spark of Deity, struck from the fire of his eternal blaze, and brought forth in the midst of eternal burning?" ("Origin and Destiny of Woman," in *The Vision*, N.B. Lundwall, comp. [Salt Lake City: Bookcraft, n.d.] pp. 145–46.) Christ says, "I am the true light that is in you, and . . . you are in me; otherwise ye could not abound" (D&C 88:50). Christ is the *life* and the *light* of every person (see John 1:4, 9). King Benjamin teaches similarly that God preserves us from day to day, lending us breath, that we may live and move . . . even supporting us from one moment to another (see Mosiah 2:21), and that all we have and are that is good comes from him (see Mosiah 4:21).

I ask, if we live and move and have our being in him (see Acts 17:28), where is self-esteem? How do I even separate my self out from the abundant grace that makes my life and even my intellect go forward in some marvelous symbiosis with my Creator? The human self cannot be defined without putting God in the definition.

It seems obvious that we—created out of the very stuff of truth, and permeated by his power—cannot live against our own natures of light and truth and intelligence without setting up conflict and spiritual dis-ease within ourselves. Sin goes against our most essential nature. The quality of our emotional and spiritual existence is governed by divine law, and whether or not we know about these laws, or observe them, we are continually and profoundly affected by the laws of light and truth. Much of our unhappiness is self-inflicted through ignorance or through deliberate sin.

So here we have a challenging situation: a person, whose

primeval nature is truth and light and purity, begins, under the influence of a fallen environment and a fallen body, to act against his spiritual nature. His sins of ignorance or choice produce bitterness, and he begins to suffer, but usually he doesn't know what the real source of his unhappiness is. He thinks it has something to do with the people around him, or he thinks it has to do with his circumstances. We don't entirely blame him for his confusion, because of course the reason we came to earth was to learn to discern good from evil so that we could be delivered from the miserable consequences of evil and darkness (see 2 Nephi 2:26). But, as Elder Neal A. Maxwell observes, "The heaviest load we feel is often from the weight of our unkept promises and our unresolved sins, which press down relentlessly upon us" ("Murmur Not," *Ensign,* November 1989, p. 85).

Resistance to our spiritual natures manifests itself as guilt, despair, resentment, self-pity, fear, depression, feelings of victimization, fear over the scarcity of needed things, and other forms of distress. These are all functions of the fallen self and we all necessarily experience them. However, the pursuit of self-esteem will not solve the problems of the self that is in conflict because of sin or even of ignorant neglect of spiritual law.

Many people, especially children, are victimized by others. Their suffering is great and they often need much tender help and instruction in order to recover. Their understanding of who they are must be restored to them; they must be taught what the Lord Jesus Christ is offering them. Both of these healing truths are founded in faith and are processed through the Spirit. The point is that the pursuit of self-esteem will not solve the problems of those who suffer from others' sins against them.

When people are sinned against they often adopt ways of thinking and acting to defend themselves as they cope with their unhappy situations. They may learn to lie, or to try to manipulate others, or to live against their own deepest feelings of right and wrong, to blame, to resent, to resort to angry confrontations, and so on. These coping behaviors are self-defeating and increase pain. Until a person stops sinning, no matter what are

the reasons why he is sinning, no matter how innocently he
began, he cannot get entirely well (see Alma 41:15). Elder
Richard G. Scott spoke on being healed from the evil acts of
others:

> No matter what the source of difficulty and no matter how
> you begin to obtain relief—through a qualified professional
> therapist, doctor, priesthood leader, friend, concerned
> parent, or loved one—no matter how you begin, those solu-
> tions will never provide a complete answer. The final healing
> comes through faith in Jesus Christ and His teachings, with
> a broken heart and a contrite spirit and obedience to His
> commandments.
>
> . . . Do what you *can* do a step at a time. Seek to under-
> stand the principles of healing from the scriptures and
> through prayer. . . . Above all, *exercise faith in Jesus Christ.*
>   I testify that the surest, most effective, and shortest path
> to healing comes through application of the teachings of
> Jesus Christ in your life." ("To Be Healed," *Ensign,* May
> 1994, p. 9.)

The precepts of man cannot produce comprehensive healing and at best can endure only for a season (see 3 Nephi
27:11). Finally, only the actual conversion of the fallen self
through the power of the Lord Jesus Christ can rectify what is
really amiss in a human being. The angel called this fallen self
the natural man: "The natural man is an enemy to God, and
has been from the fall of Adam, and will be, forever and ever,
unless he yields to the enticings of the Holy Spirit, and putteth
off the natural man and becometh a saint through the atonement of Christ the Lord, and becometh as a child, submissive,
meek, humble, patient, full of love, willing to submit to all
things which the Lord seeth fit to inflict upon him, even as a
child doth submit to his father" (Mosiah 3:19).

Could this putting off of the natural man through the Lord
Jesus Christ actually be a recovery of our true, premortal self?

We have the account of King Benjamin's people, who,
upon hearing the word of God, became painfully conscious of

their carnal state. They cried out, "O have mercy, and apply the atoning blood of Christ that we may receive forgiveness of our sins" (Mosiah 4:2). Whereupon their sensitive souls were cleansed by the Holy Spirit, top to bottom, of all their accumulations of willfulness, disobedience, and enmity; and into that vacuum rushed the sublime love of God. They received "peace of conscience, because of [their] exceeding faith . . . in Jesus Christ." (Mosiah 4:3; is it possible that "peace of conscience" is the Lord's term for what we call self-esteem?) Perhaps these Saints had not realized just how spiritually sluggish they were until that mighty power consumed in love all their sins and their pain and their sickness and their infirmity. They became acquainted with God's goodness and tasted his love.

King Benjamin, seeing their joy, taught them how to retain it: "I would that ye should remember, and always retain in remembrance, the greatness of God, and your own nothingness, and his goodness and long-suffering towards you. . . . If ye do this ye shall always rejoice, and be filled with the love of God, and always retain a remission of your sins." (Mosiah 4:11–12.)

What does the Lord mean by the *nothingness* of man? Several scriptures describe men in this way. King Benjamin asks, "Can ye say aught of yourselves? Nay," he says. (Mosiah 2:25.) "Remember . . . your own nothingness" (Mosiah 4:11–12). Moses exclaims, "Now . . . I know that man is nothing" (Moses 1:10). Ammon says, "I know that I am nothing" (Alma 26:11–12). Alma teaches that "man had fallen and could not merit anything of himself" (Alma 22:14). Nephi exhorts us to rely wholly on the merits of Jesus Christ (see 2 Nephi 31:19). Moroni speaks of the members of the Church "relying alone upon the merits of Christ, who was the author and the finisher of their faith" (Moroni 6:4). The Savior himself declares to his Apostles, "Without me ye can do nothing" (John 15:5).

We recoil at *nothingness* because we try so hard to overcome our feelings of unimportance. But nothingness does not mean valuelessness. The Lord assures us that we are each of infinite worth to him. Rather, nothingness refers to man's fallen and reduced state in this mortal sphere (see Mosiah 4:5). Nothingness describes not man's lack of value but rather his reduced powers during his mortal probation and, especially, his all-encompassing need for the Lord. Nothingness reminds us of the reductions we voluntarily subscribed to before the foundations of this world in order to come to earth and learn how to be taught from on high.

Elder Richard G. Scott tells of a sacred experience in which strong impressions came to him during a period when he struggled to do a work the Lord had given him that was far beyond his personal capacity to fulfill. The Lord said to him, "'Testify to instruct, edify and lead others to full obedience, not to demonstrate anything of self. All who are puffed up shall be cut off.'" And then, "'You are nothing in and of yourself, Richard.' That was followed with some specific counsel on how to be a better servant." ("Acquiring Spiritual Knowledge," BYU Education Week, 17 August 1993, p. 12.)

Ammon joyfully described his own nothingness: "I do not boast in my own strength, nor in my own wisdom; but behold, my joy is full, yea, my heart is brim with joy, and I will rejoice in my God. Yea, I know that I am nothing; as to my strength I am weak; therefore I will not boast of myself, but I will boast of my God, for in his strength I can do all things." (Alma 26:11–12.) For Ammon, it seems, the whole concept of self-esteem was irrelevant. Being filled with the love of God was of far greater worth than any sense of self-confidence. If one grand objective of earth life is to gain access to the grace of Jesus Christ for our trials and divine development, we will immediately realize that self-confidence is a puny substitute for God confidence. With respect to confidence, the Lord says, "Let thy bowels . . . be full of charity towards all men . . . and let virtue garnish thy thoughts unceasingly; then shall thy confidence wax strong in the presence of God" (D&C 121:45).

Both Nephi and Mormon teach that when man is without charity he is nothing (2 Nephi 26:30; Moroni 7:44). Here we realize that as true followers of the Lord Jesus Christ we must apply for the gift of charity, which is the gift of happiness, in order that we might pass from nothingness to godliness. I am suggesting that we might want to substitute for the pursuit of self-esteem the pursuit of full discipleship with its attendant spiritual gifts, among which is the sublime spiritual gift of the pure love of Christ. Mormon wrote: "Wherefore, my beloved brethren, pray unto the Father with all the energy of heart, that ye may be filled with this love, which he hath bestowed upon all who are true followers of his Son, Jesus Christ; that ye may become the sons of God; that when he shall appear we shall be like him, for we shall see him as he is; that we may have this hope; that we may be purified even as he is pure" (Moroni 7:48).

The Lord identifies love and virtue as the essential ingredients in feelings of confidence and security. By these we dwell safely in the Holy One of Israel (see 1 Nephi 22:28). Indeed, might not the pursuit of self-confidence actually pull us away from the connection the Lord is trying to make? Might it not merely produce carnal security? (See 2 Nephi 28:21.)

It is noticeable that the pursuit of self-esteem seems to generate anxiety, while increasing humility and faith in the Lord produce consolation and rest. Mormon describes Church members who, waxing "stronger and stronger in their humility, and firmer and firmer in the faith of Christ" are filled with joy and consolation (Helaman 3:35). Alma instructs his son to teach the people to humble themselves and "to be meek and lowly in heart. . . . for such shall find rest to their souls." (Alma 37:33–34.)

Some may not like the dichotomy between the pursuit of self-esteem and faith in the Lord. Some may say that you can pursue and have both. But I do not find this idea of both pursuits in the scriptures. It seems to me that King Benjamin finds these two incompatible. He says, "Remember your own nothingness and God's goodness." In trying to have both, is there a possible double-mindedness? James says that "a double minded man is unstable in all his ways" (James 1:8). Nephi says of self-promotion: "Priestcrafts are that men preach and set themselves up for a light unto the world, that they may get gain and praise of the world; but they seek not the welfare of Zion. Behold, the Lord hath forbidden this thing; wherefore, the Lord God hath given a commandment that all men should have charity, which charity is love. And except they should have charity they were nothing." (2 Nephi 26:29–30.)

Here Nephi seems to view setting oneself up for a light to the world in order to get praise as being directly antithetical to having the pure love of Christ. One apparently can't do both. The Savior says, "Therefore, hold up your light that it may shine unto the world. Behold I am the light which ye shall hold up." (3 Nephi 18:24.) Again he says that if our eye be single to his glory, our whole bodies will be filled with light: "Therefore, sanctify yourselves that your minds become single to God, and the days will come that you shall see him." (D&C 88:67–68.) It seems as though the less attention we can give to self-esteem, the more light we can have.

Low self-esteem is often associated with feelings of incapacity, or a sense of victimization, or the realization that we can't make happen the opportunities, the approval, and the feelings that we feel we need. But our relief comes when we realize that God has limited our powers so that as we cleave to him he can work his mighty miracles in our lives. Indeed, Moroni teaches that hopelessness and despair come from lack of faith in one's access to the Lord Jesus Christ (see Moroni 10:22–23).

We may think that we or some other mortal opens the necessary doors to our future, but this conclusion is an error. We ourselves do not open these doors; only the Lord does. We exercise our agency through our choices, but he retains the power to open or close the doors.

Often doors have closed before us that seemed to lead to the opportunities we thought we had to have. We may have assumed that the closed door was a reflection of some inadequacy in ourselves; but perhaps the closed door had nothing to do with whether we were good or bad or capable or incompetent. Rather, even now a loving Father shapes our path according to a prearranged, premortal covenant (see Abraham 2:8); the opening or the closing of these various doors is dependent on the Lord's perfect perception of our developmental needs. All the elements that we really need for our individual experience here, he puts onto our path. The most important things that will happen to us in this life will come to us often by no initiative of our own, but rather because he is piloting the plan. He says that he does nothing save it be for the benefit of the world (see 2 Nephi 26:24); he has promised that, if we will be faithful, all things will work together to our good in order that we may be conformed to the image of his Son (see Romans 8:28–29).

Therefore, we do not need to fear that our future lies in the fact that an authority over us plays favorites, or that a person's employer isn't well disposed toward him. Under such a belief, one might be tempted to think that only self-promotion, or image manipulation, or the compromising of what one really believes will open the doors. But even though someone in authority thinks he controls doors, there is really only one Keeper of the Gate (see 2 Nephi 9:41). "No weapon that is formed against thee shall prosper," he says. "This is the heritage of the servants of the Lord." (3 Nephi 22:17.)

Now, I ask you, as various doors open and close, as the Lord Jesus Christ orchestrates even the details of our lives, as we are obedient to him, where is the *need* to pursue self-esteem? We don't need it. Faith in the Lord Jesus Christ will take us so much farther.

Christ himself is our model where the self is concerned. He says of himself:

1. "The Son can do nothing of himself, but what he seeth the Father do; for what things soever he doeth, these also doeth the Son likewise" (John 5:19).
2. "I do nothing of myself; but as my Father hath taught me, I speak these things" (John 8:28).
3. "The words that I speak unto you I speak not of myself: but the Father that dwelleth in me, he doeth the works" (John 14:10).

Moroni wrote that the resurrected, perfected Christ spoke to him in "plain humility" (Ether 12:39). Elder Neal A. Maxwell observed that "the Savior—the brightest individual ever to walk this planet—never sought to 'prosper' or to 'conquer' 'according to his genius' and 'strength'!" (Alma 30:17.) ("Out of the Best Faculty," Annual University Conference,

Brigham Young University, 23–26 August 1993.) "Every man," Korihor taught, "fared in this life acccording to the management of the creature; therefore every man prospered according to his genius, and . . . every man conquered according to his strength" (Alma 30:17). Alma identified this precept that man prospers solely by his own resources as the doctrine of the anti-Christ.

It seems to me that the self may actually be an interloper in most of what we do and that we can find relief from the stresses and strains of self-promotion by saying, in effect, "Get thee behind me, Self." I wonder if this is what the Savior means when he says, "He who seeketh to save his life shall lose it; and he who loseth his life for my sake shall find it" (JST Matthew 10:34). The self seems to be a constant intruder as we strive for selflessness. President Ezra Taft Benson pointed out that "Christ removed self as the force in His perfect life. It was not *my* will, but *thine* be done." ("Cleansing the Inner Vessel," *Ensign,* May 1986, p. 6.)

I have become aware of how demanding of attention the self is. What a lot of prayer and deliberate living it will take for me to remove my self as the force in my life! I have become aware that all my sins rise out of the self-absorption of my heart—impulses rising like the ticking of a clock in their persistent quest for self-gratification, self-defense, and self-promotion. It seems as though a change is needed at the very fountain of my heart, out of which all thought and emotion rise. Could I actually come to the point where I could act without calculating my own self-interest all the time? Could I really live my daily life so that I was constantly listening for the Lord's will and drawing down his grace to accomplish it? And when the Lord in his mercy meshes his power with my agency and my effort and brings forth some measure of success, I ask, where is self-esteem? Where is even the *need* for self-esteem? I feel as though I just want to say instead, "Lord, increase my faith."

How then does one appropriately think about oneself? I offer you Elder F. Enzio Busche's remarks. He said: "A disciple of Christ is . . . constantly, even in the midst of all regular activities, striving all day long through silent prayer and contemplation to be in the depths of self-awareness to keep him in the state of meekness and lowliness of heart" ("Truth Is the Issue," *Ensign*, November 1993, p. 25).

It seems appropriate as well to be conscious of our preciousness to our Father, while at the same time to feel meek and lowly before his sacrifices on our behalf, his respect for us, and his continuing graciousness to us. Again, Elder Busche spoke of the point at which we realize the Lord's love: "This is the place where we suddenly see the heavens open as we feel the full impact of the love of our Heavenly Father, which fills us with indescribable joy. With this fulfillment of love in our hearts, we will never be happy anymore just by being ourselves or living our own lives. We will not be satisfied until we have surrendered our lives into the arms of the loving Christ, and until He has become the doer of all our deeds and He has become the speaker of all our words." ("Truth Is the Issue," p. 26.)

When Christ is the doer of all our deeds and the speaker of all our words, I have to ask, Where is *self*-esteem? Where is the need of self-esteem? I propose that self-esteem becomes a nonissue for the person who is perfecting his faith in the Lord Jesus Christ.

If I decide to give up some of the attention my self demands, what will I replace it with? The Lord answers, "Look unto me in every thought; doubt not, fear not" (D&C 6:36). The self is so demanding that perhaps one can only let go of the pursuit of self-promotion as one cleaves to the Lord Jesus Christ (see Omni 1:26). As with Peter walking on the water, it may be our sudden self-consciousness that will cause us to fall (see Matthew 14:28–30).

The world speaks of self-image, but Alma spoke of receiving the image of God in our countenances (see Alma 5:14). In fact, we are informed: "All those who keep his commandments shall grow up from grace to grace, and become . . . joint heirs with Jesus Christ; possessing the same mind, being transformed into the same image . . . even the express image of him who fills all in all; being filled with the fulness of his glory; and become one in him, even as the Father, Son, and Holy Spirit are one" (*Lectures on Faith* 5:2).

It seems that the perception of the self as an entity separate from God will, under the right conditions, get thinner and thinner.

President Benson pressed us to be "changed for Christ," "captained by Christ," and "consumed in Christ" ("Born of God," *Ensign*, July 1989, p. 4). We might ask, What is it that must be consumed? Maybe it is our old concept of self—the one we have learned from the precepts of men. Is it possible that the pursuit of self-esteem might delay this mighty change? Indeed, what if one ceased defining self-esteem or justifying one's pursuit of it, and just ignored it? What if, instead, one just began to obey whatever divine instruction one was not obeying, to sacrifice whatever needed sacrificing, and to consecrate whatever one was holding back? What if one just set out to "seek this Jesus"? (Ether 12:41.)

So many issues that revolve around the subject of self fade like the dew in the sun as one cultivates faith in the Savior. Without him, nothing else matters. No amount of self-esteem or of anything else can adequately fill the void.

It is possible for the self to insulate itself from the love of the Lord Jesus Christ and not know it or feel it. The Savior's love is realized only when we open to the Spirit of the Lord through prayer and obedience. Otherwise, the thing we crave most, the *experience* of God's love, remains a hidden mystery. But no matter who we are or what we have done, we can repent, and may with full assurance seek to be clasped in the arms of Jesus.

The model for man's flourishing is in the scriptures. There we learn that, by ourselves, without Christ in our lives, we will feel the sorrows of the uncomforted, natural man. But with the Lord Jesus Christ, we will flourish. One who practices faith in the Lord Jesus Christ, and teaches others to do so also, will find relief from the stresses and anxieties of the pursuit of self-esteem.

CHAPTER FOUR

Premortal Election and Grace

The world finds God's election of Israel inexplicable, but it would not do for the covenant people themselves to misunderstand their own election. The reason for Israel's election has important implications for us during our mortal probation.

Here is one oft-cited passage from Deuteronomy reflecting God's reasons for the election. Moses proclaimed to Israel: "For thou art an holy people unto the Lord thy God: the Lord thy God hath chosen thee to be a special people unto himself, above all people that are upon the face of the earth. The Lord did not set his love upon you, nor choose you, because ye were more in number than any people; for ye were the fewest of all people: But because the Lord loved you, and because he would keep the oath which he had sworn unto your fathers." (Deuteronomy 7:6–8.) What is the meaning of God's love for Israel?

In his writings the Apostle Paul made several references to Israel's election, indicating that God called Israel in the premortal world and foreordained them to exaltation (see Ephesians 1:3–5, 11–12; 2 Timothy 1:9; Romans 8:29; 9:10–12, 17). The well-known passage in Jeremiah speaks on a more individual level: "Before I formed thee in the belly I knew thee; and before thou camest forth out of the womb I sanctified thee" (Jeremiah 1:5). Joseph Smith adds to this insight, "Every man who has a calling to minister to the inhabitants of the world was ordained to that very purpose in the Grand Council of heaven before this world was" (*Teachings of the Prophet Joseph Smith*, comp. Joseph Fielding Smith [Salt Lake City: Deseret Book, 1977] p. 365; hereafter cited as *TPJS*). The Lord has told us very little of what happened in the premortal world, but piecing together some of what has been revealed through scripture and latter-day prophets causes a misty scene to come into sharper focus and provides us with insights that have power to strengthen our faith in the Lord Jesus Christ and to transform our lives.

What can we discover about the events that transpired in the premortal world that have such great implications for us here? Several enlightening scenes appear. In the beginning, the Grand Council of Gods convened to present the plan of salvation to the spirit children. The plan required that man condescend to an earth where his memory of his faculties and glorious condition in the premortal life would be veiled. Elder Parley P. Pratt wrote of the veiling, suggesting also a reduction in man's spiritual condition during mortality: "During his [man's] progress in the flesh, the Holy Spirit may gradually awaken his faculties; and in a dream or vision, or by the spirit of prophecy, reveal, or rather awaken, the memory to a partial vision or to a dim and half-defined recollection of the intelligence of the past. He sees in part and he knows in part; but never while tabernacled in mortal flesh will he fully awake to the intelligence of his former estate. It surpasses his comprehension, is unspeakable, and even unlawful to be uttered." (*Key to the Science of Theology* [Salt Lake City: Deseret Book, 1978], p. 31.)

President Brigham Young remarked on the nature of man's condescension: "It seems to be absolutely necessary in the providence of Him who created us, and who organized and fashioned all things according to His wisdom, that man must descend below all things. It is written of the Savior in the Bible that he descended below all things that he might ascend above all. Is it not so with every man? Certainly it is. It is fit then that we should descend below all things and come up gradually, and learn a little now and again, receive 'line upon line, precept upon precept, here a little and there a little.'" (*Journal of Discourses* 15:3; hereafter cited as *JD*.)

Elder John A. Widtsoe wrote, elaborating further on this condescension and perhaps suggesting some apprehension among the spirits about their coming to mortality: "They [mankind] would go to the earth in forgetfulness of the past . . . to be clothed in bodies of 'earth-element,'. . . subject to the conditions of earth, instead of the perfected state of their spirit home. More terrifying was another requirement. Sometime in their earth career their earth-bodies would be separated from their spirit-bodies, a process called death. . . . To subject an eternal being to the dominion of 'earth element'—that is, to forgetfulness, the many vicissitudes of earth, and eventual death—appeared to be a descent in power and station. . . . Man, made to walk upright, must bend his back through the tunnel through the mountain which leads to a beautiful valley. Adam and Eve accepted the call to initiate the plan, and subjected themselves to earth conditions." (*Evidences and Reconciliations,* comp. G. Homer Durham [Salt Lake City: Bookcraft, 1960], pp. 73–74.)

In speaking of the "congeniality of spirits," and thus by inference of the reductions that man would experience in this mortal sphere, Joseph F. Smith wrote: "I think that the spirit, before and after this probation, possesses greater facilities, aye, manifold greater, for the acquisition of knowledge, than while manacled and shut up in the prison-house of mortality." President Smith continued: "Had we not known before we came the necessity of our coming, the importance of obtaining tabernacles, the glory to be achieved in posterity, the grand object to be attained by being tried and tested—weighed in the balance, in the exercise of the divine attributes, god-like powers and free agency with which we are endowed; whereby, after descending below all things, Christ-like, we might ascend above all things, and become like our Father, Mother and Elder Brother, Almighty and Eternal!—we never would have come; that is, if we could have stayed away." (*Gospel Doctrine* [Salt Lake City: Deseret Book, 1977], p. 13.)

President Smith also wrote that while yet in the premortal life we knew much of what lay before us in mortality, just as the Savior did: "Can we know anything here that we did not know before we came? . . . I believe that our Savior is the ever-living example to all flesh in all these things. He no doubt possessed a foreknowledge of all the vicissitudes through which he would have to pass in the mortal tabernacle, when the foundations of this earth were laid, 'when the morning stars sang together, and all the sons of God shouted for joy.'. . . And yet, to accomplish the ultimatum of his previous existence, and consummate the grand and glorious object of his being, and the salvation of his infinite brotherhood, he had to come and take upon him flesh. He is our example. . . . If Christ knew beforehand, so did we. But in coming here, we forgot all, that our agency might be free indeed, to choose good or evil." (*Gospel Doctrine*, p. 13.)

Elder Orson Pratt wrote of yet another prospect that would not have appealed to us: "Spirits, though pure and innocent, before they entered the body, would become contaminated by entering a fallen tabernacle; not contaminated by their own sins, but by their connection with a body brought into the world by the fall, earthly, fallen, imperfect, and corrupt in its nature. A spirit, having entered such a tabernacle, though it may commit no personal sins, is unfit to return again into the presence of a holy Being, unless there is an atonement made." (Orson Pratt, "The Pre-existence of Man," *The Seer*, July 1853, p. 98; see also Mosiah 3:16.)

Although we "shouted for joy" (Job 38:7) at the prospect of continuing our progress to our exaltation, is it possible that the contamination of the heavier "earth element," the slower spiritual faculties, the assurance that we would all sin—is it possible that all these perceived sacrifices and reductions produced among the spirit host a sense of vulnerability and fear? Perhaps this is the Apostle Paul's meaning where he seems to say that only our premortal hope in Christ made it possible for us to condescend to the "bondage of corruption," knowing that Christ would deliver us "into the glorious liberty of the children of God" (Romans 8:20–21).

What was the nature of that hope? As we well know, the divine premortal plan provided for a Savior. "Whom shall I send?" the Lord asked (Abraham 3:27). Jesus volunteered to be that Savior, endorsing the Father's plan. Satan then offered himself—and a radical modification of the plan. The Prophet Joseph Smith described the circumstances: "The contention in heaven was—Jesus said there would be certain souls that would not be saved; and the devil said he could save them all, and laid his plans before the Grand Council, who gave their vote in favor of Jesus Christ" (*TPJS*, p. 357).

As Jesus Christ stood before the spirit congregation in his intelligence and love and majesty, well known to the spirit host, some readily exercised faith and others would not.

We remember that faith is a principle of power in every estate, not just on earth. God himself exercises faith to bring to pass and uphold his creations (see Hebrews 11:3; explained in *Lectures on Faith* 1:14–17). Faith in any sphere is a reward for personal righteousness. We may assume that many of the spirit children who exercised faith in Jesus Christ had already had much experience in obeying and searching out divine law in the premortal world, and to them, faith in God's revelations came easily. Thus, two-thirds exercised varying degrees of faith in the yet unrealized promises of Jesus Christ. The Prophet said, "At the first organization in heaven we were all present, and saw the Savior chosen and appointed and the plan of salvation made, and we sanctioned it" (*TPJS*, p. 181).

Presumably it was clear to every spirit among those two-thirds that each one's personal success ultimately depended not only on one's own choices but also on the love, will, power, and constancy of the appointed Savior. It was clear that, spiritually speaking, we would have to rely wholly on the merits of the Savior (see 2 Nephi 31:19; Moroni 6:4; John 15:5).

We might wonder whether Satan's success with one-third of the spirit host (see D&C 29:36) was not a function of fear at the prospect of earth life. Were the necessary reductions and sacrifices so fearful to them that a large portion of the entire spirit host preferred to abort their eternal progression so as not to have to confront earth life in the flesh at all? Did Satan, sensing his political opportunity, capitalize on their fear of the seemingly overwhelming conditions of a fallen world and propose changes in the Father's plan such that no one would have had to exercise faith, rely on grace, or suffer reductions and sacrifice? President John Taylor adds the further insight that Satan wanted to deprive man of his agency so that he, the supposed redeemer, would not have to be subject to man:

> Satan . . . wanted to deprive man of his agency, for if man had his agency, it would seem that necessarily the Lord would be subject to him [man]; as is stated, "For it behooveth the Great Creator that he suffereth himself to become subject unto man in the flesh, and die for all men, that all men might become subject unto him" [2 Nephi 9:5–7].
>
> The Lord being thus subjected to man, He would be placed in the lowest position to which it was possible for Him to descend; because of the weakness, the corruption and the fallibility of human nature. But if man had his free agency, this necessarily would be the result, and hence, as it is said, Jesus descended below all things that He might be raised above all things; and hence also, while Satan's calculation was to deprive man of his free agency, and to prevent himself or the Only Begotten from being subject to this humiliation and infamy, the Lord's plan was to give man his free agency, provide a redeemer, and suffer that redeemer to endure all the results incidental to such a position, and thus,

by offering himself as a substitute and conquering death, hell and the grave, he would ultimately subjugate all things unto himself; and at the same time make it possible for man to obtain an exaltation that he never could have had without his agency. (*The Mediation and Atonement* [Salt Lake City: Deseret News Co., 1882], p. 142.)

Whatever the issues, a terrible war ensued. President Brigham Young taught with respect to that war that "the Lord Almighty suffered this schism in heaven to see what his subjects would do preparatory to their coming to this earth" (*JD* 14:93). It seems that the Lord allowed the conflict as a sifting of and a preparation for the spirit children. We gained experience in that conflict that would work to our advantage in our mortal probation.

Out of that two-thirds of the spirit children who supported the Lord Jesus Christ's messiahship, it seems likely that a smaller group distinguished themselves by their valiance in the War in Heaven over the issues concerning the plan of salvation (see Alma 13:3) and by their exceeding faith in the premortal promises of the Lord Jesus Christ, and that this valiant group became the covenant people, or premortal Israel. Elder Bruce R. McConkie explained: "Israel is an eternal people. She came into being as a chosen and separate congregation before the foundations of the earth were laid; she was a distinct and a peculiar people in preexistence, even as she is in this sphere. Her numbers were known before their mortal birth, and the very land surface of the earth was 'divided to the nations [for] their inheritance' (Deuteronomy 32:8)." (*A New Witness for the Articles of Faith* [Salt Lake City: Deseret Book, 1985], pp. 510–11.)

Elder Melvin J. Ballard said that premortal Israel was "a group of souls tested, tried, and proven before they were born into the world. . . . Through this lineage were to come the true and tried souls that had demonstrated their righteousness in the spirit world before they came here." (*Crusader for Righteousness* [Salt Lake City: Bookcraft, 1966], pp. 218–19.)

Alma explained: "This is the manner after which they were ordained—being called and prepared from the foundation of the world according to the foreknowledge of God, on account of their exceeding faith and good works; in the first place [the premortal world] being left to choose good or evil; therefore they having chosen good [e.g., the Lord Jesus Christ and the plan of salvation], and exercising exceedingly great faith, are called with a holy calling" (Alma 13:3).

Because of their exceeding faith in the Lord Jesus Christ and their desires to promote his work on the earth, this premortal group of covenant people were elected to receive extensive grace on the earth in order to accomplish their own Christlike missions. I suggest that this is one meaning behind the Apostle Paul's use of the term "election of grace" (Romans 11:5); that is, that premortal Israel was elected to receive extensive grace in their mortal probation.

It might be helpful to point out a distinction here in the possible meanings of grace. The LDS Bible Dictionary says that grace means divine help, necessary help, divine enabling power that one cannot provide for oneself. Sometimes, as with resurrection, grace is given regardless of worthiness; but much grace is given based on exceeding faith and faithfulness.

The issue of grace brings us to the main question of this section: What indeed were the promises of the Lord to his spirit brothers and sisters that gave us courage to come to earth? They are all comprehended in the word *grace*. We are born without a conscious memory of these promises, but the Lord has supplied scripture and personal revelation to restore in some measure our premortal memories so that we can act in faith in this mortal probation as we did in the premortal world.

Amidst the premortal events, as we have seen, the covenanting spirits were foreordained to exaltation. Calling and election, based on faith in the Lord Jesus Christ, was extended to the covenant people. Paul speaks of this premortal promise in this passage: "God hath from the beginning chosen you to salvation [or exaltation] through sanctification of the Spirit and belief of the truth. Whereunto he called you by our gospel, to the obtaining of the glory of our Lord Jesus Christ" (2 Thessalonians 2:13–14). As Paul teaches here, the calling and election to exaltation made in the premortal world was not to be automatically granted, but would come "through sanctification of the Spirit." That is, the tabernacled spirits would have to make their calling and election sure on earth by standing in their premortal covenant with Jesus Christ through baptism, receiving the Holy Ghost, and pursuing sanctification until they received the more sure word of prophecy (see D&C 131:5).

It is important to note that *foreordination* does not imply the Calvinistic notion of *predestination,* which term acknowledges no necessary worthiness on the part of those predestined to be saved. Clearly, any members of modern Israel could at any point throw the premortal plan away, fall short of their promised glory, and fail to make their premortal calling and election sure.

Consider this next passage not only for its promise but also for its end result: "And we know that all things work together for good to them that love God, to them who are the called according to his purpose. For whom he did foreknow, he also did predestinate [Greek *foreordain*] to be conformed to the image of his Son" (Romans 8:28–29). In this passage Paul teaches the working together for good, or an orchestration of events, for those who love God and were premortally called to assist in the great work of the salvation of men. This promise of orchestration of life events must have been among the most compelling for us. It might be restated in this way: a plan with strongly programmed elements would operate for each covenant person, so that each could have the opportunities necessary to save himself or herself through the continually accessible grace of Christ and, in addition, have a saving influence on as many other people as possible (see D&C 86:8–11; 103:9–10). These programmed elements include the following:

1. *Chosen lineage, time, place, family, and so forth.* That some kind of organizing power brooded over the families of the earth is clear when one reads that Adam prophesied concerning and Enoch beheld all the families of the earth (see Moses 5:10; 7:45).

President Harold B. Lee taught: "You have been blessed to

have a physical body because of your obedience to certain commandments in that premortal state. You are now born into a family to which you have come, into the nations through which you have come, as a reward for the kind of lives you lived before you came here and at a time in the world's history, as the Apostle Paul taught the men of Athens [Acts 17:26] and as the Lord revealed to Moses, determined by the faithfulness of each of those who lived before this world was created." ("Understanding Who We Are Brings Self-Respect," *Ensign*, January 1974, p. 5.)

The covenant spirits would be born through a chosen lineage that has the right to the priesthood, an essential and powerful form of grace. This lineage, of course, began with Adam but was carefully funneled through subsequent selected lines until it came to Abraham, Isaac, and then Jacob, who was renamed Israel. Covenant Israel, or the members of the Church of Jesus Christ today, possess the literal blood of Abraham, Isaac, and Jacob in their veins (see Abraham 2:10–11; D&C 86:8–11). Some have called this "believing blood."

With the promise of blood lineage comes an additional blessing. Jehovah says to Abraham, "I know the end from the beginning; therefore my hand shall be over thee" (Abraham 2:8).

Not only was the lineage selected, but also the time and place, the family, and the order of birth, so that each spirit would have that unique configuration of experiences necessary for his or her particular divine needs, including membership in the Church. This careful placement of a person into the temporal house of Israel is part of the election of grace (see D&C 84:99; Romans 11:5–7; LDS Bible Dictionary, "Grace").

In connection with this grace of chosen lineage and birth circumstances, God provided yet a further complex of blessings to give every spirit the greatest possible power to obtain exaltation. I want to focus closely now on one specific, also very encouraging and liberating, form of grace:

2. *Individually orchestrated life events.* I shall address this section somewhat more personally. I catch myself saying in this

telestial world, "I am afraid of this happening," or "What if that happens, then such and such will happen." I hear my loved ones projecting fear into the future and I realize that some of us are either just uninformed concerning our privileges as covenant people or are spiritually careless with what we do know. So I am advocating an *informed* faith—not just wishful thinking that hopes that everything will work out okay, but real faith based on an understanding of the express teachings of the Lord Jesus Christ.

There is a troublesome question that the premortal covenant of grace answers: Is the universe random? Can just anything happen to us or our loved ones when random events mesh to produce catastrophe, and we are caught in the middle? As we sense our personal vulnerability in a world of overwhelming forces, we are susceptible to a telestial view that the whole cosmos is out of control and that just anything *could* happen. When we are operating under a telestial perception, we can easily feel victimized by the seemingly uncontrollable powers of nature and the malignant agency of men and by that terrifying word *accident*. It can seem as though we were cast out of the premortal existence like so many random dice into an earthly game of "whose agency could ruin whose life?" We may even fear that the great God of heaven and earth wound up the whole creation like a clock and either went off to do something else while we ran down, or at best is only intermittently accessible. Or perhaps he has sat around helplessly, restrained by some omnipotent law of agency, beholding the mess that man would make.

But let us, who tend to get caught up in patterns of worry, reconsider three principles from scripture.

God is perfectly omniscient. Many scriptures make it abundantly clear that there is not anything that God does not know (see, for example, 2 Nephi 9:20; 2 Nephi 27:10; D&C 130:7; Moses 1:6; 1:27–28). Elder Neal A. Maxwell observed: "God's omniscience is *not* solely a function of prolonged and discerning familiarity with us—but of the stunning reality that the past and present and future are part of an 'eternal now' with God!

(Joseph Smith, *History of the Church* 4:597). . . . For God to foresee is not to cause or even to desire a particular occurrence—but it is to take that occurrence into account beforehand, so that divine reckoning folds it into the unfolding purposes of God. . . . God has foreseen what we will do and has taken our decision into account (in composite with all others), so that His purposes are not frustrated." (*All These Things Shall Give Thee Experience*, pp. 8, 12.)

God is omnipotent. He has power to prevent or produce any event. The Lord's power is "over all the inhabitants of the earth" (1 Nephi 1:14); "the Lord is able to do all things according to his will" (1 Nephi 7:12); the Lord has "all power unto the fulfilling of all his words" (1 Nephi 9:6); "by the power of his almighty word [God] can cause the earth [to] pass away" (1 Nephi 17:46); God is "the all-powerful Creator of heaven and earth" (Jacob 2:5); and so on. *Lectures on Faith* reinforce God's power over all things to make salvation possible: "Unless God had power over all things and was able, by his power, to control all things, and thereby deliver his creatures who put their trust in him from the power of all beings that might seek their destruction, whether in heaven, on earth, or in hell, men could not be saved" (4:12).

God is emotionally committed to his children. "For behold, this is my work and my glory—to bring to pass the immortality and eternal life of man" (Moses 1:39). God has invested his godly heart and his mighty resources in causing things to work together for man's greatest blessing; in fact, "He doeth not anything save it be for the benefit of the world; for he loveth the world, even that he layeth down his own life that he may draw all men unto him" (2 Nephi 26:24).

From the foregoing truths, that God is omniscient, omnipotent, and fully committed to us, we may conclude as follows: The fact that mankind's agency operates on the earth does not require a creation that is out of control. The truth is that men choose what they will do, but God limits or extends, or orchestrates their choices into his great overarching purposes for his children. He works through natural or spiritual law to see that his purposes are fulfilled. Man's choices are necessarily restricted in order to protect the universe; still, man has that amount of agency necessary either to be damned or to be exalted.

Man's choices are circumscribed by the type of kingdom he lives in. He must remain within the bounds in which the Lord has placed him (see D&C 88:38). He only exceeds telestial bounds through exercising terrestrial or celestial principles. We are invited to exceed our telestial bounds through making a connection with the laws and powers of Jesus Christ.

When a person makes a covenant with the Lord Jesus Christ to obey his commandments and to strive for true and honest discipleship, a whole set of transcendent laws comes into play for that person: "That which is governed by law [the law of Christ] is also preserved by law and perfected and sanctified by the same. That which breaketh a law [the law of Christ], and abideth not by law, but seeketh to become a law unto itself, and willeth to abide in sin, and altogether abideth in sin, cannot be sanctified by law, neither by mercy, justice, nor judgment." (D&C 88:34–35.) Heavenly Father's laws are very powerful and are a great gift to us, because when we take care to obey them, these divine laws are activated to preserve us and prosper us (see Psalm 121:4, 8; 37:23). Our obedience to the laws and ordinances of the gospel lifts us above a seemingly random-event universe and puts us in a situation where we may dwell safely in the Holy One of Israel (see 1 Nephi 22:28). But he warns: "I, the Lord, am bound when ye do what I say; but when ye do not what I say, ye have no promise" (D&C 82:10).

However, as we well know, election to grace will not preclude bad things from happening to good people. Nephi says of himself in the very first verse of the Book of Mormon, "Having seen many afflictions in the course of my days, nevertheless, [I have] been highly favored of the Lord in all my days" (1 Nephi 1:1). Even though, as part of our divine curriculum, we are called to go through different kinds of affliction (see D&C 122:5–7), these are often lightened by the Lord because of our covenant relationship with him. The Lord speaks to Alma's people in their afflictions: "Lift up your heads and be of good comfort, for I know of the covenant which ye have made unto me. . . . I will . . . ease the burdens which are put upon your shoulders, that even you cannot feel them upon your backs, even while ye are in bondage; and this will I do that ye may stand as witnesses for me hereafter, and that ye may know of a surety that I, the Lord God, do visit my people in their afflictions. (Mosiah 24:13–14; see also Alma 33:23; 38:5.)

With this informed and restored faith, we, the covenant people, can rest, like Jesus, while the tempest rages (see Matthew 8:24). God will "wake us" if we need to be wakened; God will bring to our attention that which it is necessary for us to know when we need to know it. He may also withhold certain information so as to precipitate a situation which is pregnant with learning possibilities for us. The right orchestration, the right timing for events, even sad ones, is part of the covenant promise—if we hold up our end of the covenant as best we can. Maybe we can even give up the phrase, "If I had only known!"

Even one's appointed days on the earth are known beforehand by the Lord. Elder Neal A. Maxwell wrote: "The lifespans of planets, as well as prophets, are known to God; the former pass away by his word. (Moses 1:35.) To a suffering Joseph Smith, God said, 'Thy days are known, and thy years shall not be numbered less.' (D&C 122:9.) Such a promise could not have been made if all other things that bore upon the lifespan of Joseph Smith were not also known beforehand to God—in perfectness." (*All These Things Shall Give Thee Experience*, p. 13.) The Psalmist wrote: "All the days ordained for me were written in thy book before one of them came to be" (Psalm 139:16, NIV version; see also Alma 40:10; Helaman 8:8; D&C 42:48; 63:3; 121:25; Acts 17:26; Isaiah 38:5). President Ezra Taft Benson, speaking at President Spencer W. Kimball's funeral, said: "It has been said that the death of a righteous man is never untimely because our Father sets the time. I believe that with all my soul." ("Spencer W. Kimball: A Star of the First Magnitude," *Ensign*, December 1985, p. 33.)

When we covenant with the Lord Jesus Christ we become passengers on a plan that moves steadily toward its destiny in the celestial kingdom, with all the sights, sensations, relationships, and experiences particularly selected for our personal, most effective use of this preparatory period. Elder Richard Scott said: "He would have you suffer no consequence, no challenge, endure no burden that is superfluous to your good" ("Obtaining Help from the Lord," *Ensign,* November 1991, p. 86). We may know then for ourselves that what is coming in our individual futures is benign in its design if we will pay attention to the lesson it means to impart and be faithful to the Lord.

Therefore we can go about our business (see D&C 98:14; 122:9) and not fear that some random event will arrest our forward progress to our spiritual destiny. The Lord reassures us: "The works, and the designs, and the purposes of God cannot be frustrated, neither can they come to naught. . . . Remember, remember that it is not the work of God that is frustrated, but the work of men." (D&C 3:1, 3.)

One might be tempted to think that if God knows everything that we will do, if the plan is already in place, maybe we can just quit trying and let everything unfold without our own effort. But we must keep in mind that, in some way that is perhaps beyond the finite mind to understand, two things are true at once: God knows it all, but we must strive to our very utmost to make the plan work for our eternal development. The principle is something like the axiom that we must pray as though everything depended on the Lord, but work as though everything depended on us.

Latter-day Saints are premortal Israel, come to earth. It was our premortal faith in all this that gave us the courage to come to this life in the first place. Wouldn't it be a shame if we failed to grasp all that has been put in place for our blessing during our mortal probation? In this life Satan succeeds in ruling over many people by fear, as he did in the premortal world. Our faith in our election to grace can replace our telestial fears. The

Apostle Paul reminds Israel that "the just shall live by faith" (Romans 1:17). And with his great faith the Prophet Joseph Smith gave the Saints of his day counsel that is equally appropriate to us today: "Therefore, dearly beloved brethren, let us cheerfully do all things that lie in our power; and then may we stand still, with the utmost assurance, to see the salvation of God, and for his arm to be revealed" (D&C 123:17).

CHAPTER FIVE

Women, Priesthood, and the At-One-Ment

Women frequently ask, "Why do the scriptures seem to present women as second-class citizens?" The question may reveal a need for a larger view of the nature of maleness and femaleness. Men and women exist in relationship to each other. Here is one scripture that illuminates the divine relationship possible between men and women: "And I, the Lord God, caused a deep sleep to fall upon Adam; and he slept, and I took of one of his ribs and closed up the flesh in the stead thereof; and the rib which I, the Lord God, had taken from man, made I a woman, and brought her unto the man. And Adam said: This I know now is bone of my bones, and flesh of my flesh; she shall be called Woman because she was taken out of man. Therefore shall a man leave his father and his mother, and shall cleave unto his wife; and they shall be one flesh." (Moses 3:21–25; see also Matthew 19:4–6.)

This figurative account of the creation of man and woman reveals the wholeness that is intended for them. From one they came, and to eternal at-one-ment they are to return. A closer look at the Hebrew text reveals that the woman is not to be understood as inferior to the man; she is, according to the Hebrew in Genesis 2:18, a partner worthy of him. The King James Version English tends to obscure the meaning. The Hebrew word for *helper* connotes not an assistant of lesser status, nor a subordinate, nor an inferior, but one who is at least an equal. The Hebrew has the sense of "corresponding to" (see footnote to Genesis 2:18 in LDS Bible). Adam reacts with delight when he sees Eve, for she is a cherished part of himself, without whom he felt alone and bereft. Paradise was meaningless without her—"bone of my bones, flesh of my flesh" (Genesis 2:23). This phrase is idiomatic, meaning: "one of us," in effect, "our equal" (see R. David Freedman, "Woman, A Power Equal to Man," in *Biblical Archaeology Review*, January/February 1983, p. 58).

In Genesis 2:18 the Lord says, in essence, that Adam and Eve were created equal and complementary—that is, each completes the other in the eternal scheme. Thus, from oneness they came, to oneness they are foreordained to return through the power of the Atonement—or more expressly, the at-one-ment—in Jesus Christ. The insight here is that, because God saw them as equal and complementary, he gave them equal and complementary, but not identical, work to do.

Spencer W. Kimball wrote:

We had full equality as his spirit children. We have equality as recipients of God's perfected love for each of us. . . . Within those great assurances, however, our roles and assignments differ. These are eternal differences—with women being given many tremendous responsibilities of motherhood and sisterhood and men being given the tremendous responsibilities of fatherhood and the priesthood—but the man is not without the woman nor the woman without the man in the Lord (see 1 Corinthians

11:11). Both a righteous man and a righteous woman are a blessing to all those their lives touch.

Remember, in the world before we came here, faithful women were given certain assignments while faithful men were foreordained to certain priesthood tasks. While we do not now remember the particulars, this does not alter the glorious reality of what we once agreed to. (*The Teachings of Spencer W. Kimball,* ed. Edward L. Kimball [Salt Lake City: Bookcraft, 1982], pp. 315–16.)

The symbolism of deriving the woman from the man, rather than making the woman a separate creation, emphasizes not her secondary quality but rather the couple's primeval unity and eternal wholeness as future gods. Erastus Snow spoke of the man and woman united in godhood:

I sometimes illustrate this matter by taking up a pair of shears . . . composed of two halves, but they are necessarily parts, one of another, and to perform their work for each other, as designed, they belong together, and neither one of them is fitted for the accomplishment of their works alone. And for this reason says St. Paul, "the man is not without the woman, nor the woman without the man in the Lord." In other words there can be no God except he is composed of the man and the woman united, and there is not in all the eternities that exist, nor ever will be, a God in any other way. (*JD* 19:270.)

A modern Apostle, Elder James E. Talmage, wrote on the subject of eternal womanhood:

In the restored Church of Jesus Christ, the Holy Priesthood is conferred, as an individual bestowal, upon men only, and this in accordance with Divine requirement. It is not given to woman to exercise the authority of the Priesthood independently; nevertheless, in the sacred endowments . . . , woman shares with man the blessings of the

Priesthood. When the frailties and imperfections of mortality are left behind, in the glorified state of the blessed hereafter, husband and wife will administer in their respective stations, seeing and understanding alike, and co-operating to the full in the government of their family kingdom. Then shall woman be recompensed in rich measure for all the injustice that womanhood has endured in mortality. Then shall woman reign by Divine right, a queen in the resplendent realm of her glorified state, even as exalted man shall stand, priest and king unto the Most High God. Mortal eye cannot see nor mind comprehend the beauty, glory, and majesty of a righteous woman made perfect in the celestial kingdom of God. ("The Eternity of Sex," *YW Journal* 25 [October 1914], pp. 602–3; quoted in *The Words of Joseph Smith*, comp. Andrew F. Ehat and Lyndon W. Cook [Provo, Utah: Religious Studies Center, BYU, 1980], p.137, n 4.)

President Joseph Fielding Smith wrote similarly: "Women do not hold the priesthood, but if they are faithful and true, they will become priestesses and queens in the kingdom of God, and that implies that they will be given authority" (*Doctrines of Salvation,* comp. Bruce R. McConkie, 3 vols. [Salt Lake City: Bookcraft, 1956], 3:178).

The Lord's revealed order for men and women here in mortality is the preparation for that glorious day of their exercising authority in their respective stations. This current order on earth is an essential preparation for the eternal family kingdom to come.

Although women do not assume priesthood responsibilities in this life, women do have right and access to all the gifts of the Spirit. No difference in spiritual power and potential is implied by giving priesthood authority to men only. Spiritual power is based on personal sanctification, faith, and thorough submission to righteousness. These gifts are not gender specific.

The mystery of godliness is great as it pertains to men and women (Ephesians 5:31–33), and matters concerning the nature of men and women before this life have not been revealed in much detail. But since priesthood is eternal (e.g., see D&C

84:17) and gender is eternal, the relationship between men and women may be more or less the same from estate to estate. Elder Talmage wrote on the eternity of gender:

> The distinction between male and female is no condition peculiar to the relatively brief period of mortal life; it was an essential characteristic of our pre-existent state, even as it shall continue after death, in both the disembodied and resurrected states. . . .
>
> Woman occupies a position all her own in the eternal economy of the Creator; and in that position she is as truly superior to man as is he to her in his appointed place. Woman shall yet come to her own, exercising her rights and her privileges as a sanctified investiture which none shall dare profane.
>
> It is part of woman's mission in this life to occupy a secondary position of authority in the activities of the world, both in the home and in the affairs of public concern. . . . That many men fail in their station, that some are weak and unfit, that in particular instances the wife may be the more capable and in divers ways the better of the pair, should not be considered as evidencing impropriety or unrighteousness in the established order as a general condition. Woman should be regarded, not in the sense of privilege but of right, as the associate of man in the community of the home, and they two should form the governing head of the family institution, while to each separately pertain duties and functions which the other is less qualified to discharge. Weakness or inefficiency on the part of either in specified instances must not be taken to impugn the wisdom by which the organization of the home and of society has been planned. ("The Eternity of Sex," pp. 600, 602.)

Many have wondered if the events in the Garden of Eden cast women in an unfavorable light. For example, Paul wrote: "For Adam was first formed, then Eve. And Adam was not deceived, but the woman being deceived was in the transgression." (1 Timothy 2:13–14.) In what way did Eve transgress? She transgressed that law that would have sustained her forever in a terrestrial world, and she set in motion telestializing processes. Yet evidently Eve knew she had to eat the fruit in order to fulfill God's command to "be fruitful, and multiply" (Genesis 1:28) and to have her heart's desire for children, as well as her own eventual exaltation. After all, the meaning of her Hebrew name, "the mother of all living," suggested what she had come to earth to do.

Therefore, in what way might she have been deceived?

As background, we remember that it was necessary that the spirit host waiting in the premortal world descend to a lower world, a mortal state, where evil could flourish. Brigham Young said: "Darkness and sin were permitted to come on this earth. Man partook of the forbidden fruit in accordance with a plan devised from eternity, that mankind might be brought in contact with the principles and powers of darkness, that they might know the bitter and the sweet, the good and the evil, and be able to discern between light and darkness, to enable them to receive light continually." (*JD* 7:158.)

On another occasion President Young said, "Mother Eve [partook] of the forbidden fruit. We should not have been here to-day if she had not; we could never have possessed wisdom and intelligence if she had not done it. It was all in the economy of heaven. . . . When I look at the economy of heaven my heart leaps for joy, and if I had the tongue of an angel, or the tongues of the whole human family combined, I would praise God in the highest for his great wisdom and condescension in *suffering the children of men to fall into the very sin into which they had fallen,* for he did it that they, like Jesus, might descend below all things and then press forward and rise above all." (*JD* 13:145; emphasis added.)

In the scriptures, the word *know* usually suggests knowledge gained from experience, not just having information about something. To *know* evil, we had to become subject to it to some extent, as part of descending below all things. To know good and to be redeemed, we must respond to the light when, on the Lord's timetable, it is offered to us.

And so it was with Eve. Part of her tutorial in life was to learn how, in a mortal body, to discern between what was good, or of-God, and what was evil, or not-God. To make these distinctions she had to be confronted by evil, be in some way deceived by it, and become subject to it. In this and subsequent experiences she would come to know what was God from what was not God, and would come to experience the joy of her redemption (see Moses 5:11).

The Lord has not given us all the information about the events in Eden, but I suggest one possibility concerning the way in which Eve was deceived. Eve in the garden occupies a position similar to the Savior's in the wilderness when Satan tried to tempt him to turn the stones into bread. The Savior recognized Satan and refused to do his bidding with the words: "Man shall . . . live by . . . every word that proceedeth out of the mouth of God" (Matthew 4:4). Jesus refused Satan because to do what Satan bade him do would have put him in subjection to Satan, which consequence would have relieved him of his messiahship. Eve apparently did not recognize Satan and may not have understood about subjection to him. Their eating the fruit at his enticement nevertheless placed them in that subjection (see D&C 29:40). Is it possible that the deception rested in the fact that Eve took it from the wrong hand, having listened to the wrong voice?

Eve had taken an initiative that was not hers to take—alone. After all, her act would have an irreversible impact on Adam. Perhaps what Eve had to learn was to listen to the right voice, to seek the voice of righteousness before she acted. A major issue in the Garden, as in life, is, to which voice will we be subject? I am not suggesting that the events in Eden could or should have happened in any other way. These events happened just as they had to in order to subject Adam and Eve to the tutorials required for their future exaltation. Eve's being placed in a counseling role to her husband, far from being a punishment, was a sacred tutorial designed to sanctify both of them.

How could a counseling position be a sanctifying position? The very fact that the Lord put Eve in a counseling role with

Adam acknowledges eternal woman's great ability to do what needs doing. But her divine, developmental need is to act *within* a relationship, taking into account Adam's need to be part of that relationship. Each had need of the relationship—it was not good for the man [or the woman] to be alone—he needed her and she needed him. The man and the woman had become like God, and now, even though they rejoiced in the opening of their eyes and their prospects of joy (see Moses 5:10–11), they had need not to compete for ascendancy but to console each other in their mutual loss of paradise and their mutual quest to attain exaltation.

The issue here is not who is more capable, men or women, but who will do the work God has appointed. If the presiding role of priesthood is withheld from women, it is not because they could not do the work of priesthood—that they are not spiritual enough, not intelligent enough, or not rational enough—but rather to foster the conditions in which the man and the woman may achieve interdependence.

What makes all of this so hard in practice? It may seem unfair that the man is subject to a perfect head (the Lord Jesus Christ), and the woman is presided over by an imperfect head (her husband). But how much humility the man must cultivate to hear the Lord's voice! And how much humility the woman must exercise to encourage and rely on her imperfect husband to make that connection! The man's presidency over the woman is designed to be as much a tutorial for him as it is for the woman as she submits to his presidency. A very fine tuning is required of each. Some of the principles that should govern the relationship between the man and the woman might be suggested in the Lord's instruction to priesthood quorums: "The decisions of these quorums . . . are to be made in all righteousness, in holiness, and lowliness of heart, meekness and long suffering, and in faith, and virtue, and knowledge, temperance, patience, godliness, brotherly kindness and charity; because the promise is, if these things abound in them they shall not be unfruitful in the knowledge of the Lord" (D&C 107:30–31).

Elder Rulon G. Craven, who served for more than thirteen

years as secretary to the Quorum of the Twelve, made this helpful observation: "The members of the Twelve strive to live according to the promptings of the Spirit. They speak their mind.
However, they are also good listeners and speak when moved
upon by the Holy Spirit. Their posture in quorum meetings is
to listen and sense the directing power of the Spirit, which always leads to a unity of decision. I marveled as I watched the directing power of the Spirit touch the minds and hearts of the
members of the Twelve, influencing the decision-making
process. . . . They strive continually to abide by the counsel of
the Lord found in section 107, verse 30, of the Doctrine and
Covenants." ("Prophets," *Ensign*, May 1991, p. 28.)

Lines of authority belong to the pattern of the Lord for all
his people. The Lord has set each of his children, whether male
or female, in a hierarchical chain that requires each to listen
carefully to the voice of one set above him or her. Through listening to those the Lord has placed in positions of authority
and blessing, one learns how to listen to and obey the Lord.
Hierarchies of authority after the Lord's order accomplish
divine purposes when embraced and sustained.

We see that the Lord has given us the challenge of not only
perfecting ourselves individually but also perfecting ourselves in
relationships. Perfecting oneself in a relationship cannot be separated from personal perfecting.

As to perfecting ourselves in a relationship, it is easy for us
to live for a good many years on the assumption that we have a
right to be satisfied by life events and by the people in our lives.
This is a precept of man. If we continue all the way through
this life with that assumption, we will have failed to learn what
we came here to learn and will have failed to develop some personal essentials. We will never obtain the essential divine nature
and can never be exalted until we know and practice the truth.
One important truth is that our husbands, our wives, and our
children were not given to us to satisfy us, and nor were many
of the most important events of our lives. To the world, love is
a relationship in which the parties involved satisfy each other
enough that they can call that relationship "love." But this is
not love at all—it is just self-serving.

We can tell that our love is often based on the degree to which another person satisfies us: If they don't satisfy us, we criticize them. It seems to me that most criticism is saying, "In these ways, this person does not satisfy my expectations as to what he should be." But our expectations are a function of the finite mind, the telestial and selfish mind, not the mind of God. I see women who have good husbands but fail to value and nurture what they have. I myself have committed these very sins.

We stand in a sacred relationship to the people in our lives, especially family, because they are not there by chance. The people in our lives were placed there not only for us to enjoy but also to cross us and to dissatisfy us from time to time so that we can learn that love is not a matter of personal satisfaction but a going out of our hearts to empathize with, to understand, and to try to bless the other, giving up the demand of the natural man for satisfaction—to love the other, to forgive the other, to cease to demand that the other satisfy us, and to seek to be able to bless that person. Relationships were given to us to develop us in love.

I want to share what I have observed through the years, in myself and others; therefore, the perspective is from a wife's viewpoint, but the same principles apply to other relationships.

1. A woman may have decided to pit her will against her husband's will, and thereby she sets up a no-win situation for her husband. So long as the husband does not do what she wants, he cannot do right. A wife may not sense that this situation is diabolically inspired, will shred a marriage, and will preclude exaltation for the wife.

2. Some women show disdain for their husbands when their husbands do not capitulate to their will or somehow fail to sense or meet the desire in the wife's mind. This too is self-serving and diabolical in its power to destroy an otherwise exaltable marriage. They have set up the lens of dissatisfaction through which they view their husbands, often blaming their husbands for their own failure to love. This perverse way of viewing a husband can create years, even a lifetime, of cold war, silent or noisy misery, and a forever feeling of emptiness. It is one of the powers by which Satan can rule over the marriages

of the Latter-day Saints and the world too. But he has more to gain in souring a Latter-day Saint marriage because of its temporal and eternal potential.

A deeply devoted couple whose power in the Spirit is based on their mutual nurturing and giving of grace have a sanctifying influence on their children and on many more besides. They can build the kingdom of God in ways they cannot foresee. The couple's unhappiness, on the other hand, cuts short the filling of the measure of their creation.

3. Some women withhold grace from their husbands to control or manipulate or punish them. Grace is enabling or strengthening power given to another who can't provide it for himself—but needs it. A woman has a great reservoir of grace out of which she can give enabling and strengthening power to her husband—if she drops all real or imagined grievances against him and sets her heart to love and bless him, physically, emotionally, and spiritually. This is one of the most powerful but easily overlooked mysteries of godliness. The Apostle Peter has some good counsel for wives and husbands [the King James Version translation obscures the meaning a little, so I have "re-translated" somewhat]: "[Adorn your hearts with the hidden woman of the heart]—a meek and quiet spirit, which is in the sight of God of great price. For after this manner in the old time the holy women also, who trusted in God, adorned themselves, being in subjection unto their own husbands; even as Sara obeyed Abraham, calling him lord: whose daughters ye are, as long as ye do well, and are not afraid [to love your husbands or be subject to them in righteousness]. Likewise, ye husbands, dwell with [your wives] according to knowledge, giving honour unto the wife, as unto the weaker vessel, and as being heirs together of the grace of life; that your prayers be not hindered. Finally, be ye . . . of one mind, having compassion one of another . . . be pitiful, be courteous: not rendering evil for evil, or railing for railing: but contrariwise blessing; knowing that ye are thereunto called, that ye should inherit a blessing." (1 Peter 3:4–9.)

It is so easy to complicate that which is really simple. It is so easy just to love and enjoy the real beauties of life.

So women tend to compete for authority and men tend to abuse authority—hence many are called, but few are chosen (see D&C 121:39–40). As Hugh Nibley observed: "The gospel sets absolute limitations beyond which patriarchal authority may not be exercised—the least hint of unkindness acts as a circuit-breaker." ("Patriarchy and Matriarchy," in *Old Testament and Related Studies* [Salt Lake City and Provo: Deseret Book/FARMS, 1986], p. 96.) Brother Nibley points out that both patriarchy and matriarchy are apostate forms of government. Yet many men exercise their authority in unkindness; women and children are often victims of it. And many women exercise their prerogatives insensitively and leave their victims behind them. But it's so unnecessary.

In this day of the restoration of the fulness of the gospel, the Lord asks the covenant people not to embrace the world's definitions of male and female roles or to mimic their marriages; rather, he urges them to live the order they learn in the temple endowment and in temple marriage. The point of putting the woman in a counseling role to the man is that as both of them strive for something higher than themselves, their relationship will not founder in a power struggle but will flower in mutual support and in spiritual growth for each. The point of giving priesthood authority to only one of two imperfect people is to create interdependence and at-one-ment between them. The point of the Adam and Eve relationship is to return the man and the woman to at-one-ment before the Lord. Thus we can foil the powers that seek to tear the man and woman asunder.

CHAPTER SIX

Enduring Marriage

It is true that there are marriages that are disasters, in which the best thing a partner can do is to get out as soon as possible; where to remain would mean the emotional or even physical destruction of that partner. In these situations, divorce can be a blessing. But a great many divorces today do not arise from the gross unrighteousness of the partners; rather, they happen because one or the other fails to understand, or comes to reject, the nature and purpose of true marriage. Here I want to make some observations exclusively on that garden-variety Latter-day Saint marriage where two ordinary, good people fall in love and get married. What follows is to be understood in the context of two good people, not in the context of an abusive marriage.

It could be that the initial love that prompts us to marry is a bit self-serving. This immature love may tend to wear off as the challenges of life assail the marriage. Therefore, at some point in nearly every marriage, one or the other partner may think that he or she is falling out of love. Perhaps the other one is not meeting his expectations anymore; perhaps little obnoxious traits overshadow the once highly valued traits of the spouse. Perhaps she married in the first place looking for someone who would cherish her deeply and anticipate her every need. Or maybe she married to shape her companion into an image of what she thought he should be. Whatever the mistaken notion, a spouse may start looking for someone who will better fill his or her expectations, usually of sexual love or romance.

But the hope of making a better match is an illusion because, unless the other spouse is guilty of serious sin, the real problem is in the dissatisfied partner. His search for something better reveals a mistaken approach to marriage. He is focusing on what he wants out of the marriage (over which he may have little control), rather than what he has failed to put into it. He may think he has lost the "feeling" of love, but true love is not governed by feeling. The person who truly loves does so because he or she chooses to love. True love is a decision.

We don't want to ask for too much in a mate, but we also don't want to settle for too little. Of course we have expectations for the one we marry: we are becoming a team to accomplish holy things, to embark on a holy endeavor. In the courting process we are looking for certain traits: responsibility, fidelity, cleanness, considerateness, and so on, as well as romantic love. We want the whole package, and that isn't too much to ask for people who want eternal marriage. But the major question must be, given these initial qualities, Is this a person I want to love by nurturing him and compassionately seeing him through his development and problems, whatever the course of time may show them to be? If the answer is a sober "yes," and the marriage is contracted, the ongoing question becomes, How can I truly love and nurture my mate?

This person one chooses to marry doesn't have to be one's "soulmate." President Spencer W. Kimball taught:

While marriage is difficult, and discordant and frustrated marriages are common, yet real, lasting happiness is possible, and marriage can be more an exultant ecstasy than the human mind can conceive. This is within the reach of every couple, every person. "Soulmates" are fiction and an illusion; and while every young man and young woman will seek with all diligence and prayerfulness to find a mate with whom life can be most compatible and beautiful, yet it is certain that almost any good man and good woman can have happiness and a successful marriage if both are willing to pay the price. (Spencer W. Kimball, *Marriage,* [Salt Lake City: Deseret Book, 1978], pp. 37–38.)

The Lord commands—in true marriage—that two people, imperfect, quite different from each other (no matter how much they may have in common), learn to triumph over their differences through tolerance and kindness, and learn, struggling together with spiritual principles, what it means to be one. Oneness, by the way, doesn't mean thinking and feeling the same way about everything; rather, it has to do with being dedicated to encouraging one another's spiritual growth, having reverence for one another's individuality, and coming together into oneness of heart with the Lord's purposes. True marriage is spiritually based.

We may have hoped by finding a "soulmate" to gain confirmation of what we already are when we marry. But what we need when we marry is to develop along lines we may not yet foresee. Thus instead of marrying a soulmate we marry a unique person and embark on learning to *become* a soulmate, since few are ready to have, or be, soulmates when they marry.

We cannot depend on the physical relationship to solve all our problems. This relationship is truly important to marriage. Elder Boyd K. Packer calls the power of procreation the key to the plan of happiness (see "The Fountain of Life," Brigham Young University 18–Stake Fireside, 29 March 1992); but it does not in itself make husband and wife one. Sex can be a lonely experience when there are no other facets of oneness in the marriage. Instead, it is devotion to God's will that finally teaches the couple oneness; then all other aspects can come into harmony.

A successful marriage in the Lord's definition, that marriage which merits sealing by the Holy Spirit of Promise, is never a casual achievement or a stroke of luck. It is always a triumph of spiritual principles, a product of selfless, sustained effort on behalf of both partners, a victory arising out of the will to love: the will to extend oneself to encourage one's own or another's spiritual growth. This victory comes often with the sacrifice of one's own convenience or desires.

Few of us enter marriage prepared to nurture another. We learn it out of a desire to live the gospel, to love the Lord, and to love our partner. The practice of true love is an act of self-development (see Alma 41:14–15). We make a lot of mistakes in the process because we are not used to extending such selfless effort. Almost nothing has prepared us for it before marriage. But out of the pain of our repented-of mistakes, out of much practice, we learn the peace and achieve the richness of love.

God designed marriage as a refuge—two people tenderly caring for each other through life's experiences—but also as a tutorial in love. Each has something to teach the other, and the learning is usually not easy. If marriage is not seen as a tutorial in love, a preparation for living in eternity, Satan can rend the marriage by causing the partners to focus on what is unimportant and on the ever-dangerous goal of self-fulfillment. From a small seed of self-seeking—diabolical discontent—an otherwise promising marriage can end in sorrow or limp along in misery for years. The misery is unnecessary, because, with right understanding, it is easy just to love and to bless. Our spouse was not given to us necessarily to satisfy us, but for us to love.

And so marriage, perhaps more than any other relationship—because it is more intimate than any other—is our greatest spiritual challenge and has the greatest potential, along with parenthood, to make godly beings of us. We must leave off trying to perfect our spouse and study how best to apply the principles of love in ourselves. Marriage may be one of our greatest tutorials in perfecting love in ourselves. One's exceedingly great kindness to one's spouse will bear rich fruit in mutual tender feelings.

Marriage is a contract to nurture another person forever, because nurturing is the work of gods. Jesus said to the Pharisees, "What therefore God hath joined together, let not man put asunder. . . . Moses because of the hardness of your hearts suffered you to put away your wives; but from the beginning it was not so." (Matthew 19:6, 8.)

Eternal marriage is both a type and a function of the Savior's at-one-ment. Therefore, eternal marriage, like so many other divine achievements, is a function of grace. That is, married love that endures is a gift of the Spirit (see Moroni 7:48).

The moment when a partner fears that he or she may have fallen out of love with the other partner is the moment when the opportunity for genuine love begins. It is perhaps the moment when a readiness for a step up in spiritual maturation has arrived. It is the moment when we realize what great power we have to bless the person to whom we are married, and how much power we have to cause unnecessary pain.

Shall we commit the ultimate selfish act and abandon spouse and children in the search for another partner, shattering trust and breaking the hearts of many, in the hopes of some greater fulfillment in love? This is a phantom desire, born of deception. What a tragedy such a decision is, since the only fulfillment one can ever have is that arising out of righteousness!

The restless partner must look, then, at the ways in which he could restore and enrich the original love, nurture his spouse, and unlock the blessings of heaven on the marriage. Is this hard work? Does this mean total repentance—letting go of favorite grudges, forgiving, humbling oneself, sacrificing the satisfaction of "being right"? Yes! But my witness is that there are special blessings reserved for those who devote themselves to making marriage work, blessings that are realized in this life and in the life to come: hidden treasures of the Spirit, reserved for those who would be gods.

CHAPTER SEVEN

Love and Fear

"There is no fear in love; but perfect love casteth out fear: because fear hath torment. He that feareth is not made perfect in love." (1 John 4:18.)

My remarks here deal rather one-sidedly with the idea that mothers are not entirely responsible for the way their children turn out, for good or for ill. In spite of my weaknesses as a mother, I have wonderful children. Obviously a mother has power to do her children a lot of good. But here I want to discuss mothering that has not been perfect, a kind of mothering we may all have done. How may a woman who fears that she has made serious mistakes with her children, or maybe with anyone she has loved, enter into the rest of the Lord? This chapter concerns parental love and fear.

I come from a family of wonderful people who nevertheless struggled with how to be happy. There were many things we didn't know about living in peace. We mixed our love with fear.

My brilliant father suffered from alcoholism, and we all suffered with him. He too had come from a troubled family. He gave up alcohol and made significant strides before he died, but what I experienced in my childhood family seemed to color my life with confusion.

I joined the Church at nineteen. Though my conversion was real, many of my emotions continued to be out of harmony with gospel teachings, and I didn't know what to do about them. I was not at rest. As a young mother I felt that I was only barely keeping my distress from leaking out. But it did leak out. I struggled to be cheerful at home. I was too often tense with my children, especially as their behavior reflected negatively on me. I was perfectionistic. I was irritable and controlling. But I was also loving, patient, appreciative, happy; I frequently felt the Spirit of the Lord, and I did many parenting things well, but so inconsistently. How could I dissolve this shadow self and become fully resonant with gospel teachings?

Sooner or later the crisis comes for good people who live in ignorance and neglect of spiritual law. The old ways don't work anymore, and it may feel as though the foundations of life are giving way. After some nineteen years of motherhood, my poor over-controlled children seemed like enemies, I was a workaholic, I was exhausted, and I had no idea where to go for help. I wanted peace.

Finally the day came when I knew I had to have help. During a very tearful, pleading prayer, the Lord spoke to me clearly: "Go home." I made arrangements to fly back to my parents' home, where my father had just finished an intensive rehabilitation program for recovering alcoholics. That drying-out process had gone on before, but this time there was something different. The program reached out to help all the members of the alcoholic's family, most of whom are troubled and need help until they know who they are, why they feel as they do, and what to do about it.

At home I attended a four-hour orientation program for children and spouses of alcoholics. I read books on being an alcoholic child, I talked to other alcoholics who had become counsellors in this rehabilitation program, and I didn't stop praying. I could tell that I was on the verge of re-creation.

I have found since then that if we don't learn consistent, mature love in our childhood homes we often struggle to learn it when we become marriage partners and parents. Many people who did not come out of alcoholic families nevertheless suffer from the same kinds of distress as I did. Apparently it doesn't matter what the manifest problem was in the child's family, but in a home where a child is emotionally deprived for one reason or another that child will take some personal emotional confusion into his or her adult life. We may spin our spiritual wheels in trying to make up for childhood's personal losses, looking for compensation in the wrong places and despairing that we can find it. But the significance of spiritual *rebirth* through Jesus Christ is that we can mature spiritually under his parenting and receive healing compensation for these childhood deprivations.

Three emotions that often grow all out of proportion in the emotionally deprived child are fear, guilt, and anger. The fear grows out of the child's awareness of the uncontrollable nature of her fearful environment, of overwhelming negative forces around her. Her guilt, her profound feelings of inadequacy, intensify when she is not able to make the family situation better, when she is unable to put right what is wrong, either in the environment or in another person, no matter how hard she tries to be good. If only she could try harder or be better, she could correct what is wrong, she thinks. She may carry this guilt all her life, not knowing where it comes from, but just always feeling guilty. She often feels too sorry for something she has done that was really not all that serious. Her anger comes from her frustration, perceived deprivation, and the resultant self-pity. She has picked up an anger habit and doesn't know how much trouble it is causing her.

A fourth problem often follows in the wake of the big three: the need to control others and manipulate events in order to feel secure in her own world, to hold her world together—to *make* happen what she wants to happen. Here is

ignorance of the reality of God's power to hold the universe together. She thinks she has to run everything. She may enter
adulthood with an illusion of power and a sense of authority to
put other people right, though she has had little success at it.
She thinks that all she has to do is try harder, be worthier, and
then she can change, perfect, and save other people. But she is
in the dark about what really needs changing.

As my own part in my distress began to dawn on me, I
thought I would drown in guilt and wanted to fix all the people
that I had affected so negatively. But I learned that I had to
focus on getting well and leave off trying to cure anyone
around me! Many of those around me might indeed get better
too, since we seldom see how much we are a key part of a negative relationship pattern. I have learned that it is a true principle
that I needed to fix myself before I could begin to be truly
helpful to anyone else; I began to understand motes and beams
(see Matthew 7:5).

I learned the serenity prayer: "God grant me the serenity to
accept the things I cannot change, courage to change the
things I can, and wisdom to know the difference." I used to
think that if I were worthy enough and worked hard enough,
and exercised enough anxiety (which is not the same thing as
faith), I could change anything. But I learned that my power
and my control were illusions. I learned that to survive emotionally I had to turn my life over to the care of that tender
Heavenly Father who was really in charge. I learned that it was
my own spiritual superficiality that was making me sick, and
that only profound repentance, that real change of heart,
would ultimately heal me. My Savior was much closer than I
had dreamed and was willing to take over the direction of my
life: "I am the vine, ye are the branches: He that abideth in me,
and I in him, the same bringeth forth much fruit: for without
me, ye can do nothing" (John 15.5). My brain knew these
truths, but to my heart they were new insights.

The crisis I'd precipitated with my violations of eternal law
also provided moments of blazing insight. As the old foundations crumbled, I felt terribly vulnerable. I learned that much

humility and prayer and flexibility are the keys to passing through this corridor of healthy change while we experiment with truer ways of dealing with life. I learned things, as Moses did, that I never before had supposed (see Moses 1:10). Godly knowledge, lovingly imparted, began deep healing for me, gave me tools to live by and new ways to understand the gospel. "If thou shalt ask, thou shalt receive revelation upon revelation, knowledge upon knowledge, that thou mayest know the mysteries and peaceable things—that which bringeth joy, that which bringeth life eternal" (D&C 42:61). Here, for example, are some peaceable things I learned:

First, each parent brings to her parenting personal weaknesses which will provide opposition for her children. Although we do not want to be the source of even a part of our children's opposition, most of us are, in one way or another. That is a sobering observation, though not surprising. But we remember that God knew ahead of time the failings, the confusions, misunderstandings, weaknesses, and spiritual infirmities of each of his children. With this knowledge he prepared the gospel plan. He allowed us the experiences of mortality, providing certain compensations and blessings and talents which would present themselves as we struggled with the opposition along life's path.

Many of us parents bring out of our childhood some consequences of our own parents' spiritual infirmities. Of course, we are only describing the conditions of a fallen world—it is a world of weakness and infirmity, but it is also a divinely sanctioned learning environment for this stage in our eternal development. Perhaps one of the most important views of life to embrace is that this life is a series of tutorials designed to give us experience, to develop the divine nature, and to send us to the Lord Jesus Christ, the Master Teacher and Keeper of Grace. So it has seemed to me that parenthood may be designed at least as much for parents as for children.

Again, I do not want to diminish the fact that a mother can do much necessary good for her child, but why do some of us learn valuable parenting lessons after it seems mostly too late to incorporate them? Perhaps because it is never too late, really, in the eternal scheme of things. It seems that when Mother gets better, everyone in the family gets better—no matter how old the children are.

Second, children's personalities are not created by their parents; they have their own unique personality chemistry, which they bring from the premortal life. Much of this personality formation exists beyond the parents' control. What the child chooses to do is a unique reaction between his own personality, his agency, and his environment. Thus some children out of the seemingly best environments have serious problems, while others out of very deprived environments may show amazing maturity and resilience.

As children grow, they gradually become responsible for what they do with the opposition in their lives. I mentioned earlier that although children are born to imperfect or even emotionally sick parents, they have access to divine resources to help them overcome and benefit from their imperfect environment. For example, they may have counterbalancing spiritual gifts, character traits, blessings, or solutions that will present themselves on life's path again and again as they grow. The children then gradually become responsible to partake of those solutions that the Savior offers them individually.

As solutions become apparent, we as parents may find ourselves in a difficult situation: We think we have produced trouble in a child's life. We now think we know what the solution is. We want to undo the trouble. We offer our best solution. We may be right or we may be wrong, but we want that child to apply the solutions we think he needs—right now. It is very frustrating when a child will not. We find we cannot undo the trouble as soon as we want it undone. We learn that no child of any age can be forced to accept solutions. The child may even prefer the trouble to the solution. Parents can pray for, but must also wait for, readiness in a child. We learn divine patience, coming to understand our eternally patient Savior more and more.

In the meantime it is helpful to remember that as a child makes mistakes and lives with the consequences he is gaining experience. Even if he seems to be living in terrible danger of one kind or another, he exists in a universe overseen by an omnipotent and loving God on whom nothing is lost.

One of our problems is that we feel so responsible. Latter-day Saints are very responsible people. Perhaps some of us assume more responsibility than is ours; we may even try to assume God's responsibility. We may think we bear the whole load of another's salvation and forget that every person is a child of God and has his own personal Savior. I learned that I am not my loved ones' Savior. Love may easily turn into unrighteous dominion, into interference with a plan that must unfold between a person and his Savior. When love tries to control, it is not love, but fear. I am trying to resist the temptation to control the choices my loved ones make.

Third, no mother, not even a sick mother, can deprive her child of the celestial kingdom. A person's exaltation is ultimately his own responsibility, not his mother's. Women may give lip-service to the principle that we are finally responsible only for our own salvation, but in the same moment we may be filled with the terrible fear that we have failed our children irreparably. There seems no restitution we can make. Fortunately, we are wrong. Restitution comes in the mother's healing process. We must avoid thinking that our children's salvation rests solely on us. We are but one component in a multi-faceted plan.

Fourth, with all our hearts we do not want to be the cause of suffering; but where suffering is inevitable, we find solace in the knowledge that all people must suffer in order to learn life's greatest teachings. People have a right, even a need, to suffer. Suffering will often propel us to God, where we learn life's most precious mysteries. We may forever try to get between our children and their painful experiences, whether we created the pain or not. But there are some lessons that only pain can teach, and for us to try to remove all pain is beyond our stewardship and control, especially the pain of consequences for sin. We may thwart the plan of God by trying to remove consequences.

So we learn to be wiser than we have been and to go in a direction that we had never before thought to go: we let go and let God. We learn patience and faith in the unfolding of an individual plan for each of our children.

Fifth, many mothers have had children who have experimented with a few things. These mothers have agonized. They have stormed the gates of heaven. They have cajoled. They have taught until the children were sick of Mother and the gospel. They have reproached, they have pleaded, they have threatened. These mothers can learn: love must be governed by intelligence, patience, and faith, not anxious emotion. Jacob says, "I will unfold this mystery unto you; if I do not, by any means, get shaken from my firmness in the Spirit, and stumble because of my over anxiety for you" (Jacob 4:18). Over-anxiety can actually block the Spirit. Maybe that's why the Savior of the world reminds us, "Be still, and know that I am God" (Psalm 46:10).

It is very hard to let go of that agonizing knot in the intestines that urges us to take all the blame and to beat ourselves mercilessly. But if we are going to learn godliness we must redirect the energy that we're giving to sick anxiety over another's choices. We do not perfect others with our fear, or even with our love; rather, we perfect the principle of love in ourselves.

To our children there may be something unwholesome about our love if they feel too much anxiety in it. They may feel they are being manipulated by our so-called love. They don't receive it as love, and perhaps they are right. Rather than love, it may be more like fear, or hurt pride, or anger over failure to control. They must see that our happiness is not dependent on their conversion. We must take care not to try to manipulate them with our unhappiness.

Rather, as God is at peace in spite of our choices, so may we be at peace in spite of anyone else's choices. Alma tells his wayward son, Corianton, that the nature of God is a state of happiness (see Alma 41:11). One's nature can be independent of what others do. "All truth is independent in that sphere in which God has placed it, to act for itself, as all intelligence also" (D&C 93:30).

Shall we destroy ourselves with grief and self-reproach? Does God destroy himself over the choices of his children? Surely not; otherwise the celestial kingdom would have no peace for us. We do not struggle to gain our exaltation just so

we can suffer on a grander scale. Do we love our children more
if we allow our grief over them to destroy us? Do we love them
less if we allow them their agency and establish serenity in our
own bosoms? Can we actually detach ourselves from the
tyranny of our grief? If we are going to be gods, we must realize that our loved ones are independent agents; we must get
used to people rejecting our best gifts.

As I think about serenity, or the Lord's rest, in my own
bosom, I consider these scriptures:

— Alma 33:23: "And then may God grant unto you that
your burdens may be light, through the joy of his Son.
And even all this can ye do if ye will." If we will cast our
burdens on the Lord, as he invites us to do, and not
cling like martyrs to them, we will find relief. I ask myself, "Why am I hurting myself?" God doesn't ask me to.
Just the opposite. Perhaps I have liked thinking that my
anxiety was a measure of my spiritual sensitivity or my
love, but I have had to admit that really it was either
neurosis or lack of faith, or both.

— Moroni 7:3: "Wherefore, I would speak unto you that
are of the church, that are the peaceable followers of
Christ, and that have obtained a sufficient hope by
which ye can enter into the rest of the Lord, from this
time henceforth until ye shall rest with him in heaven."
Mormon observes that the Church members to whom
he is speaking have already entered into the Lord's rest.
Did their right to God's rest mean that they didn't have
difficult children or errant loved ones, that they had
never made mistakes and therefore could enter into the
rest of the Lord? I am learning that my rest in God is
not dependent on others' choices, not even my children's. It is dependent on my own repentance and my
implementation of saner principles.

— D&C 6:36: "Look unto me in every thought; doubt not,
fear not." "Pray always, and I will pour out my spirit
upon you, and great shall be your blessing. . . . Yea, come
unto me thy Savior" (D&C 19:38, 41). Prayer has brought
many a wiser parent, and then even her wayward child,

home again. The Lord Jesus Christ is described as being full of grace and truth (2 Nephi 2:6). A reservoir of grace abounds in our Savior that can be tapped for our families if we will learn how to gain access to it.

God lives. An attentive Savior lives who is willing to take loving charge in the life of each of us. There are divine solutions to each of our most distressing dilemmas. There are principles to learn and to work by. There is restitution. We may indeed cast out fear, and love with serenity.

CHAPTER EIGHT

Living the Spirit of At-One-Ment

The Lord Jesus Christ's atonement for you and me made possible an at-one-ment society. The spirit of the Lord's at-one-ment is always seeking access to our relationships, but this spirit can seem very elusive in our personal and business worlds. The world we live in seems to have little relationship to a Zion society. Nevertheless, the powers in the Atonement apply to our lives right now and are accessible to you and me right now. These powers have implications for every relationship we have and in every combination of people we find ourselves with. They have implications for what we think and say, what we do, and how we feel. These powers may hold the secret to making right relationships endure and may help us to know what is wrong with potentially good relationships that are going wrong.

What are the principles on which a Zion society or a community of at-one-ment is established? First we need a little background on the word *atonement. Atonement,* or *at-one-ment,* is a word introduced into English in 1526 by William Tyndale as he translated the Greek New Testament into English; specifically he created the word *at-one-ment* to translate the Greek word for *reconciliation* or *to come back into a relationship after a period of estrangement.* The scriptures tell us that man came from a heavenly society and fell, by his birth, into a state of spiritual death (see Helaman 14:16), alienated from his Heavenly Father by the nature of the Fall. Christ wrought the Atonement to restore us to the heavenly society. So we might say that the word rendered *atonement* by the early biblical translators could have been more accurately rendered *re-at-one-ment* or *reunion.* Christ wrought the great Reunion.

Scriptural uses of *atonement* or at-one-ment suggest that Christ is going to bring us to oneness in heaven and to that social harmony that we experienced before the world was, a harmony, in fact, which still continues in heaven, and into which you and I seek to be reintegrated. Joseph Smith spoke of a future "sociality coupled with eternal glory" (D&C 130:2). We have imprinted on our spirits the experiences from the premortal heavenly sociality, but we do not remember the details of our lives there. Parley P. Pratt wrote that, after God's spirit children were born, they were "matured in the heavenly mansions, trained in the school of love in the family circle, and amid the most tender embraces of parental and fraternal affection: . . . [Each spirit] lived and moved as a free and rational intelligence, acting upon its own agency . . . independent in its own sphere." (Parley P. Pratt, *Key to the Science of Theology,* p. 31.)

Since earth life and sociality is a shadow of the premortal world, we want to identify those principles that will endure into the eternal world and try to implement them here. Therefore we might observe: Things must be done on earth as they are done in heaven so that that which is earthly may be made heavenly. That which does not try to be heavenly must remain telestial and cannot be made heavenly or celestial.

At-one-ment is the condition in which heavenly beings live. If we want to live there with them, we need to practice here and now the manner of emotional and spiritual life that they live. *This* life is the time for men to prepare to meet God (see Alma 34:32). We want to think through how to live the spirit of at-one-ment and bring it to pass in whichever ways we can on the earth. I think we feel the Holy Spirit already working on us to do that, but we don't always know how to respond to the promptings.

Speaking of those with whom he will one day "drink of the fruit of the vine . . . on the earth," the Lord included those "unto whom I have committed the keys of my kingdom, and a dispensation of the gospel for the last times; and for the fulness of times, in the which I will gather together in one all things, both which are in heaven, and which are on earth; and also . . . all those whom my Father hath given me out of the world." (D&C 27:5, 13–14.)

We notice while studying scripture that it is full of references to being one, to crying with one voice to the Lord, to being of one heart and one mind. These references to oneness suggest that the spirit of at-one-ment is working upon the people and blessing and saving them. The scriptures have many at-one-ment words: oneness, in one, unity, united order, gathering (versus scattering), equal, cleave, seal, welding link, embrace, consecration, temple marriage, resurrection.

We do the work of at-one-ment in the temple when we seal our ancestors and posterity to us in great family chains. In fact, in a sense *at-one-ment* is just another word for sealing. Essential to effective prayer in the temple are feelings of love. What is the temple endowment itself but a progressive sealing of ourselves to the Lord until we are clasped in the arms of Jesus (see Mormon 5:11). Considering how comprehensive the Lord's at-one-ment work is, we can see that it is physical, emotional, and spiritual.

Most of all, we want to understand how the at-one-ment translates to personal relationships, since the ordinances we receive in the temple are inextricably linked with the principles of love and at-one-ment. We learn there that spirituality and spiritual gifts cannot be separated from loving behavior and feelings. The reason is that both of these things are attributes of godliness, and neither exists without the other.

We remember the Zion society that resulted from the Lord's visit to the Nephites:

> And they had all things common among them; therefore there were not rich and poor, bond and free, but they were all made free, and partakers of the heavenly gift. . . .
>
> And it came to pass that there was no contention in the land, because of the love of God which did dwell in the hearts of the people.
>
> And there were no envyings, nor strifes, nor tumults, nor whoredoms, nor lyings, nor murders, nor any manner of lasciviousness; and surely there could not be a happier people among all the people who had been created by the hand of God.
>
> . . . They were in one, the children of Christ and heirs to the kingdom of God.
>
> And how blessed were they! (4 Nephi 1:3, 15–18.)

How do we get to the heavenly Zion condition described in 4 Nephi? How do we learn how to live the spirit of the at-one-ment? How do we bridge the gap between where we may now perceive ourselves to be spiritually and where we want to be? Will the Lord do something magical to us to make us ready for his coming, to make us ready to build Zion, to enter at last into the kingdom of God? How do we get there from here?

I suggest that one reason why we have come to earth is to learn the principles of peace and at-one-ment in the face of considerable opposition, and to take them with us into the kingdom. We knew these principles in the premortal world, but here we may have forgotten how they work.

When we think how easily in past times we may have traded the spirit of at-one-ment for disturbance, we see what a challenge it might be for us to live in a Zion or heavenly condition where everyone will have learned, by desire and practice, to prefer the spirit of at-one-ment with each other to that of conflict or disturbance.

What is the nature of the negative energy that leads to conflict around us? It is un-peace, unrest, caused perhaps by trying to impose one's own will on others, or by criticism, anger, irritability, selfishness, failure to forgive, failure to revere another's agency, retaliation, moodiness, fear, worry, or simply forgetting to have faith in the Lord Jesus Christ. All of these we have probably all experimented with to learn bitter and sweet. These are ways most of us act until we learn that there is a better way.

We all feel negative emotions, and sometimes they need to be expressed—carefully. But even when these negative-energy emotions are fully justified, they can constitute a spiritual burden for ourselves and those around us if they are indulged in too long. Our bad temper and bad moods can become a form of abuse for us and those around us.

It may take more than a little humility to accept this truth. Perhaps we have not fully processed the idea that peace is a vital state for the Spirit to flourish in. We may not have realized the spiritual value of inner peace. Nevertheless, the Lord invites us to live in peace (see Mosiah 4:13). Mormon speaks to the peaceable followers of Christ, whom he recognizes because of their peaceable walk with men, people who have entered into the rest of the Lord (see Moroni 7:3–4).

As I have watched myself and others, it is sobering to realize how readily we trade inner peace for something less, for some sort of upset; how readily we take offense and then escalate the disturbance around us—in home or office or even church. How easily we have unsatisfied expectations of how others should treat us or what they should be doing for us—and we grow cold or irritable to retaliate for this real or imagined slight! How eagerly we may insist on being right at the expense of precious relationships! Thus keeping the water rippling around us with negative energy, we are often not still and at rest in the principles of tolerance and love, of overlooking, of letting go, of forgiving.

I find that when I am not at peace inside, I make trouble around me. I even look for trouble, picking at this, complaining at that, practicing abuse. I may yield to self-pity that causes me to withdraw, licking my wounds, waiting for someone to put right what is really my responsibility to correct inside myself. I think self-pity may be a sin because it functions to violate the spirit of at-one-ment and the power of faith. I have asked myself, How long could I last in Zion? How long would it be before I singlehandedly dismantled Zion?

Maybe I have thought that at the last judgment someone would wave a magic priesthood wand over me and I would suddenly acquire a heavenly personality. But it's clear to me now that the Lord expects me to practice here and to involve him in helping me in these kinds of personal challenges until the heavenly personality becomes mine.

A Zion society is the product of the personal choice of every person in it; it is also a function of the grace of the Lord Jesus Christ that shapes hearts to be like his. But first it begins with an individual choice, and this must become independent of others' choices for something less. I have come to know that in any moment what I send out is my choice, and I can't blame it on a situation or on another person. That personal responsibility is made very clear repeatedly in the Book of Mormon: "And now remember, remember, my brethren, that whosoever perisheth, perisheth unto himself; and whosoever doeth iniquity, doeth it unto himself; for behold, ye are free; ye are permitted to act for yourselves; for behold, God hath given unto you a knowledge and he hath made you free. He hath given unto you that ye might know good from evil, and he hath given unto you that ye might choose life or death; and ye can do good and be restored unto that which is good, or have that which is good restored unto you; or ye can do evil, and have that which is evil restored unto you." (Helaman 14:30–31.)

There is of course a power of evil that opposes at-one-ment. We mortals are not alone on this planet. The Apostle Paul wrote: "Put on the whole armour of God, that ye may be able to stand against the wiles of the devil. For we wrestle not against flesh and blood, but against principalities, against powers, against the rulers of the darkness of this world." (Ephesians 6:11–12.) Brigham Young said in connection with the subtle works of Satan: "There are thousands of plans which the enemy of all righteousness employs to decoy the hearts of the people away from righteousness" (*JD* 3:194). Joseph Smith focused the idea: "The policy of the wicked spirit is to separate what God has joined together, and unite what He [God] has separated, which the devil has succeeded in doing to admiration in the present state of society" (*TPJS*, p. 103).

Satan seeks to rend the Saints' relationships—their marriages, their family feeling, their ward associations, their business connections—so that Zion cannot be established. We forget in the very moment that we ought not that Satan and his followers promote contention (see 3 Nephi 11:29) by stirring around in the pride in the Saints' hearts. Consider these eye-opening scriptures:

— "But, O my people, beware lest there shall arise contentions among you, and ye list to obey the evil spirit" (Mosiah 2:32).

— "And [Alma] commanded them that there should be no contention one with another, but that they should look forward . . . having their hearts knit together in unity and in love" (Mosiah 18:21).

— "But behold, this was a critical time for such contentions to be among the people of Nephi. . . . It was [Moroni's] first care to put an end to such contentions and dissensions among the people; for behold, this had been hitherto a cause of all their destruction." (Alma 51:9, 16.)

— "And many more things did the people imagine up in their hearts, which were foolish and vain; and they were much disturbed, for Satan did stir them up to do iniquity continually; yea, he did go about spreading rumors and contentions . . . that he might harden the hearts of the people against that which was good" (Helaman 16:22).

— "For verily, verily I say unto you, he that hath the spirit of contention is not of me, but is of the devil, who is the father of contention, and he stirreth up the hearts of men to contend with anger, one with another" (3 Nephi 11:29).

— "I . . . establish my gospel, that there may not be so much contention; yea, Satan doth stir up the hearts of the people to contention" (D&C 10:63).

— "There were jarrings, and contentions, and envyings, and strifes, and lustful and covetous desires among them [the Saints]; therefore by these things they polluted their inheritances. They were slow to hearken unto the voice of the Lord their God; therefore, the Lord their God is slow to hearken unto their prayers, to answer them in the day of their trouble." (D&C 101:6–7.)

— "Cease to contend one with another; cease to speak evil one of another. . . . and let your words tend to edifying one another." (D&C 136:23–24.)

— "And now my beloved brethren, I would exhort you to have patience, and that ye bear with all manner of afflictions; that ye do not revile against those who do cast you out . . . , lest ye become sinners like unto them; but that ye have patience, and bear with those afflictions, with a firm hope that ye shall one day rest from all your afflictions." (Alma 34:40–41.)

— "We must attend to the ordinance of washing of feet . . . It is calculated to unite our hearts, that we may be one in feeling and sentiment, and that our faith may be strong, so that Satan cannot overthrow us, nor have any power over us here. . . . Do not watch for iniquity in each other, if you do you will not get an endowment, for God will not bestow it on such. But if we are faithful, and live by every word that proceeds forth from the mouth of God, I will venture to prophesy that we shall get a blessing that will be worth remembering, if we should live as long as John the Revelator." (Joseph Smith, *TPJS*, p. 91.)

Having discerned Satan, then, we can thwart the evil spirit in many ways. You and I have been endowed with the divine power to generate positive energy—mentally, physically, and spiritually—by carefully choosing attitudes, actions, and words according to the teachings of the scriptures. We can choose to generate positive, spiritual energy, to which the Spirit of the Lord is attracted, with which he connects, and which he magnifies for good. Thus we learn to work as the Savior works and to become as he is, even as we walk this life.

But we may have many misconceptions about how to be happy and how to establish relationships of at-one-ment with others. We may think these relationships would have to be ideal; we may think that the people around us would have to be ideal, that they would have to feel and think the way we do in order to be happy, or that we have to think as they do in order to have the spirit of at-one-ment between us. We may feel that many of the people around us do not value what we do, do not meet our hopes and dreams, and we may despair that we will ever experience at-one-ment with some of the people God has put into our lives.

Here indeed is the reality of telestial living—nearly every day someone will do to us one or more of the following: belittle, be insensitive to needs, show indifference, make us feel insecure, humiliate, frighten, abuse, inconvenience, demand, criticize, disappoint, lie, hurt, betray, try to seduce, misunderstand, resent, threaten, attack (verbally or physically).

So what shall we do about all that? What if we knew that what we do is very important—that we can't, before God, blame our response on what others do to us? What if the revelation came to us that, in fact, our earth-life experiences were designed, even fabricated, to make those abrasive experiences possible, as a sort of laboratory in which we could work out our salvation? It is in these daily abrasions that we find the imperfections in our own souls.

Maybe the purpose for such experiences can be answered with this question: How shall we ever learn Christ-like love unless we have a chance to practice it in the face of the opposites? Every disrupted relationship, whether in our own home or within a particular group or community, is a chance to forge the divine nature in ourselves and prepare for that endless state of happiness.

It would appear that all the people in our lives are there for important reasons. We stand in a sacred relationship to them because we and they cannot be made perfect without each other. Nevertheless, we remember that seldom are they given to us primarily to satisfy us. Rather, they are given to us to make possible a much greater love than we would have been capable of in a situation where everybody agreed with us, everybody loved us, everybody saw everything the way we do. These abrasive people in our lives are friends in disguise. They are there to teach us to perfect love in ourselves, not to perfect them. We don't need ideal relationships in order to be happy; we can live happily with less than ideal because each relationship can be enriched with that spirit of at-one-ment which so greatly improves the quality of our personal emotional lives.

All of us have experienced or are now experiencing troubled relationships. But I know from my own experience that miracles very often happen in troubled relationships. I grew up in a troubled family; each of the people in that family was and is a good person. They were good people with very little understanding in those early years of how to be happy. In a troubled family one may learn a number of counterproductive behaviors: to try to control others; to be critical in order to feel more secure in one's own self-righteousness; to require satisfaction from others' behavior; to use anger as manipulation; to be very self-assertive; to try to prove oneself right in every situation; to make trouble by letting people know the various ways in which they are not meeting one's expectations; to get even by using irritability, cold silences, or not-so subtle barbed words; to nag people and try to talk them into things. The people one treats in these ways come to feel they are one's enemies. Often we create these enemies within our own family circle. The results of these behaviors are that one experiences a lot of unfocused fear, tendencies to depression, guilt, and feelings that life is meaningless.

I didn't know that there was really anything wrong with me as I practiced some of these ways of treating people, but I didn't feel good. I didn't know how good I could feel. But when I began to taste the Spirit, I could feel the effects it was having on my emotions, how they were clearing up, how life was smoothing out, how sweet some moments in life were starting to be. But we try a lot of unproductive things before we find this happiness.

Here is one of the main points I want to make about our establishing Zion: I did not see a relationship between the way I treated other people and the way I felt inside: I thought that what they were doing made me unhappy, but actually it was how I was reacting and how I was interpreting the experience and what I was doing that made me unhappy. Is it possible that much of the emotional pain we have doesn't come from the love we weren't given in the past, but from the love we ourselves aren't giving in the present?

President James E. Faust said at President Howard W. Hunter's funeral that the prophet had no inner conflicts or tensions because of his humility. He was at perfect peace with himself. It made me wonder how much of our emotional turmoils are nothing more than the products of our industrial-strength pride. Alma told his son, "Teach them to never be weary of good works, but to be meek and lowly in heart; for such shall find rest to their souls" (Alma 37:34).

It is providential for us that the Book of Mormon describes some dysfunctional families and troubled relationships. Nephi, for example, lived with very abusive older brothers and experienced many abuses, received verbal and physical abuse from those who should have been his protectors and nurturers. How very relevant his experience is to so many who suffer abuse today! It appears that on several occasions he was able to forgive them frankly (see 1 Nephi 7:21).

But later he faces the debilitating effects of his brothers' behavior on himself. He is angry, only he has turned his anger inward—a very common source of depression. He sees that, although by telestial standards his anger is 100 percent justified, for his own spiritual well-being he must let it go and turn to the Lord! "Why am I angry because of my enemy? Awake my soul! No longer droop in sin. Rejoice, O my heart, and give place no more for the enemy of my soul. Do not anger again. . . . Do not slacken my strength. . . . Rejoice, O my heart, and cry unto the Lord. . . . Wilt thou make me that I may shake at the appearance of sin?" (2 Nephi 4:27–31.)

Nephi teaches this powerful principle: We are not judged for what others do to us; we are judged by *how we react* to what they do to us, based on what we understand at the time. Our happiness depends on what we do now, not so much on what was done to us.

I wish to be clear that we are not talking here about submitting to serious abuse. Forgiving people, acting kindly toward them, doesn't necessarily mean letting them abuse us. Sometimes relationships have to be severed to keep one of the parties from being destroyed. In Nephi's case, the Lord finally took him out of Laman and Lemuel's presence (see 2 Nephi 5). But Nephi waited on the Lord, teaching us that revelation is indispensable to relationship work. When we are in relationship trouble, we need to draw very close to the Lord and counsel with him as best we can (see Alma 37:37).

One additional idea: what we cannot know or remember, until the Lord reveals it, is what if anything we covenanted to do in the premortal world with respect to a particular relationship here. In some cases the Lord will take us out of a relationship, or counsel us to take ourselves out, but very often he will set about to work a small series of miracles in the relationship so that the spirit of at-one-ment can flourish in us and with us, as it does in heaven. He is trying to teach us to live in a celestial society and to master the principles that govern such a society; therefore, it seems that usually he wants us to mend rather than sever relationships. But each experience has its learnings, and when we depend on him, cleave to him, he will lead us out of even the mess we ourselves have made—wiser, one hopes, for having been through it.

Truly we receive what we send out: "For that which ye do send out shall return unto you again, and be restored" (Alma 41:15). If we don't like what we're getting in a particular relationship, we may need to check out what we're sending into that relationship.

Thoughts and feelings have energy, and they travel from their origin to affect people and things. But mostly they affect the person with whom they originated. What happens to us enters our systems as energy and takes effect through our energy systems, but what we send out in response seems to have a much more powerful effect on us (see Matthew 15:18). For example, if someone trespasses against me, I may feel a negative ripple through my system. I face the moment of decision: shall I let this assault pass out of me in intensified negative waves to my brother or sister, making a poor situation worse? Or shall I neutralize this assault by returning love, good for evil? Paul says, "Be not overcome of evil, but overcome evil with good" (Romans 12:21). The Lord teaches, "Love your enemies, bless them that curse you, do good to them that hate you, and pray for them which despitefully use you, and persecute you; that ye may be the children of your Father which is in heaven" (Matthew 5:44–45). My happiness, then, my possession of the Lord's Spirit, depends on what I decide to do among many options.

The Lord has revealed: "My disciples, in days of old, sought occasion against one another and forgave not one another in their hearts; and for this evil they were afflicted and sorely chastened. Wherefore, I say unto you that ye ought to forgive one another; for he that forgiveth not his brother his trespasses standeth condemned before the Lord; for there remaineth in him the greater sin. I, the Lord, will forgive whom I will forgive, but of you it is required to forgive all men." (D&C 64:8–10.)

The following scripture reveals the heart and core of discipleship and divine community. It is the Prophet Joseph's correction of part of the Sermon on the Mount as recorded in the King James Version of the Bible. "And unto him who smiteth thee on the cheek, offer also the other; or, in other words, it is better to offer the other, than to revile again. And him who taketh away thy cloak, forbid not to take thy coat also. For it is better that thou suffer thine enemy to take these things, than to contend with him." (JST Luke 6:29–30; see also Matthew 5:39–40.)

Joseph F. Smith comments: "His [Christ's] perfected philosophy teaches . . . that it is better to suffer wrong than to do wrong" (*Gospel Doctrine*, p. 128). That is the direction I think we want to go in our personal discipleship and in our building of Zion. In the moment that wrong is done to us, we should remember that it is better to suffer the wrong than to do wrong in our reaction. Before we react, we must ask what will best serve the cause of righteousness.

Joseph Smith's life reflects the relationship between the principles of forgiveness and the gifts of the Spirit. The following quotes David Whitmer:

He [Joseph Smith] was a religious and straightforward man. . . .He had to trust in God. He could not translate unless he was humble and possessed the right feelings towards everyone. To illustrate so you can see: One morning when he was getting ready to continue the translation, something went wrong about the house and he was put out about it. Something that Emma, his wife, had done. Oliver and I went upstairs and Joseph came up soon after to continue the translation but he could not do anything. He could not translate a single syllable. He went downstairs, out into the orchard, and made supplication to the Lord; was gone about an hour—came back to the house, and asked Emma's forgiveness and then came upstairs where we were and then the translation went on all right. He could do nothing save he was humble and faithful. (In B. H. Roberts, *Comprehensive History of the Church,* 6 vols. [Salt Lake City: Deseret News Press, 1930], 1:131.)

The Lord has forbidden getting even, paying back, taking vengeance—in any form (e.g., see Mormon 3:15). He requires us to try to act continually in a forgiving mode, being kind to those who, by the telestial way of thinking, don't deserve even a pleasant word from us.

The Lord does not mean that an offender is to get away with breaking His laws (see D&C 64:9–13). When a Church member acts in a way that could endanger his membership or breaks civil law, the offending one must come to justice for his own good and for the good of the people around him; but we are still required to forgive him in our hearts.

We know that we are required to do all that we appropriately can to promote the spiritual, emotional, and physical well-being of those the Lord has entrusted to our care. But when older children and other adults behave in ways that are very distressing to us, it is easy to become involved in ways that do not help them or ourselves. We may be so emotionally entangled that we think obsessively about what the other is doing, and this involvement only keeps us in turmoil. Sometimes our over-involvement is a blend of resentment, self-pity, and guilt. These we need to set aside. With our thoughts on bringing ourselves to the Savior, we will be less affected by what others are doing to the contrary. Thus, one who wishes to enter into at-one-ment first learns a special detachment from others whose behavior they can't control. Detaching ourselves emotionally, ceasing to manipulate the other person's life, letting that person take responsibility for his or her own behavior—this frees us from soul-sickening stress. This detachment does not imply that we withdraw our love and compassion or any appropriate help. It means that we can turn our attention to the things we have neglected, the things that truly are our concern. This special detachment produces inner serenity as we take full responsibility for what we do, repenting and correcting ourselves as necessary, and giving others responsibility for what they do. This kind of detachment is essential to any healthy relationship.

But sometimes there are effective forms of influence we haven't yet tried. "What would happen if, in our personal relationships, we just dropped all charges against those around us? What if we just happily sacrificed all bitter satisfaction, all retribution, all demand for repayment, all vengeance—we let all this go, without regret or second thoughts?" (Terry Warner, *Bonds of Anguish, Bonds of Love*, unpublished manuscript.)

Brigham Young said: "If this people would live their religion, and continue year after year to live their religion, it would not be many years before we would see eye to eye; there would be no difference of opinion, no difference of sentiment, and the veil that now hangs over our minds would become so thin that we should actually see and discern things as they are. . . . It is our privilege, for you and me to live, from this day, so that our consciences will be void of offence towards God and man; it is in our power to do so, then why don't we?" (*JD* 3:194.)

Joseph Smith said with respect to oneness:

By union of feeling we obtain power with God. . . . Nothing
is so much calculated to lead people to forsake sin as to take
them by the hand and watch over them with tenderness.
When persons manifest the least kindness and love to me, O
what power it has over my mind, while the opposite course
has a tendency to harrow up all the harsh feelings and de-
press the human mind . . . It is the doctrine of the devil to
retard the human mind and retard our progress by filling us
with self righteousness. The nearer we get to our heavenly
Father the more are we disposed to look with compassion
on perishing souls, to take them upon our shoulders and cast
their sins behind our back. . . . If you would have God have
mercy on you, have mercy on one another. (*The Words of
Joseph Smith,* comp. Andrew F. Ehat and Lyndon W. Cook
[Provo: Religious Studies Center, BYU, 1980], p. 123.)

In any encounter with any person, I can generate the spirit
of the at-one-ment through listening to him or her with empathy, through encouragement, through feeling for the Spirit
of the Lord. I can influence powerfully the atmosphere I live in
and the people I work with.
President Howard W. Hunter gives the model for working
with others:

> God's chief way of acting is by persuasion and patience
> and long-suffering, not by coercion and stark confronta-
> tion. He acts by gentle solicitation and by sweet entice-
> ment. He always acts with unfailing respect for the freedom
> and independence that we possess. He wants to help us and
> pleads for the chance to assist us, but he will not do so in
> violation of our agency. . . .
> To countermand and ultimately forbid our choices was
> Satan's way, not God's, and the Father of us all simply never
> will do that. He will, however, stand by us forever to help
> us see the right path, find the right choice, respond to the
> true voice, and feel the influence of his undeniable Spirit.
> His gentle, peaceful, powerful persuasion to do right and

find joy will be with us "so long as time shall last, or the earth shall stand, or there shall be one man upon the face thereof to be saved" (Moroni 7:36). (*Ensign*, August 1994, back page.)

Would it be an overstatement to say that during our waking hours we are generating either negative energy or positive energy? If we absolutely knew that the Lord would send his Spirit any time that we began to generate positive feeling with thoughts, words, or actions, why would we ever choose to generate something else? The Lord says, "Strengthen your brethren in all your conversation, in all your prayers, in all your exhortations, and in all your doings" (D&C 108:7).

When we live in patience and love with each other, in peace, meshing with those around us, not resisting them but supporting them, forgiving each other, speaking the words that evoke the Spirit, encouraging the positive that is in every person we know—no matter what his weaknesses—we live the spirit of at-one-ment with each other. The more we make each relationship sweeter and more tender and dear, the more we live at-one-ment. The more we lay down pride and old checklists of hurts and grievances, the more we send out healing, the more our relationships heal.

One day, when we seek, ask, and knock and the heavenly gate is opened, and we ask permission to enter, I think we will have to present something in ourselves recognizably heavenly in order to gain entrance. We have to practice at-one-ment here so that we will know how to act when we get to heaven.

"For Their Sakes I Sanctify Myself"

It is my desire to strengthen and encourage readers of this book in the quest for sanctification and in their desires to have the maximum saving influence on those around them. My assumption is that you are striving to be true disciples of Jesus Christ and are deeply interested in spiritual issues and will not be dismayed by such a discussion. It is not necessary for me to tell you that I am not a sanctified person; but I am, like you, a true seeker, and have learned some things that are changing me and strengthening my own connection to spiritual power. As a true disciple, then, what is it I have to do to get what I want—to be sanctified and to help others?

We may get confused about how to help the people we love. We may be tempted to use the spiritually unprepared, frontal approach, and then our loved ones may see our help as interference. But real help is usually accomplished after spiritual preparation and is offered gently and thoughtfully, sometimes indirectly. This help most effectively rises out of the heart that is earnestly seeking its own sanctification rather than to control or manipulate other people. It springs from an informed partnership with the Lord, from singlemindedly pursuing his will and not some personal agenda. Often the most dramatic help turns out to be some spiritual changes that we ourselves make which then bless our loved ones in unexpected ways. Thus efforts toward sanctification can be the first step in helping others.

But where the pursuit of sanctification and perfection are concerned, I wonder whether we may have thrown the baby out with the bath water. Because some have become deeply discouraged in these efforts, we may have drawn back from encouraging it. Of course we want to avoid perfectionism that is driven by ego—that kind is doomed to failure anyway. In addition, many steadily pursued sanctification efforts have foundered because the person has taken on the full burden alone; has not understood how to involve the Lord Jesus Christ, without whom the whole endeavor must break down. Here I am going to advocate a dedication to the process of sanctification that draws on spiritual forces.

My observation is that we may have set unnecessary limitations to what can be achieved spiritually. These limitations are self-imposed, not God-imposed. Through the scriptures and the Spirit, the Lord shows us what can be and draws us to that vision—and that vision is one of perfection. I don't think we should be afraid of it. What we want to know is what we have to change now to get the power to bring that vision closer to our reality. The Lord's hands are tied if we impose on him what we see as our own limitations. What we need is for him to release his power in our behalf and in behalf of our loved ones.

But as we get serious about the adventure of sanctification, we have to accept these following truths:

Said Brigham Young: "Our mortal existence is a school of experience" (*JD* 9:292).

We know the design of our Father in heaven in creating the earth and in peopling it, and bringing forth the myriads of organizations which dwell upon it. We know that all this is for His glory—to swell the eternities that are before Him with intelligent beings who are capable of enjoying the height of glory. But, before we can come in possession of this, we need large experience, and its acquisition is a slow process. Our lives here are for the purpose of acquiring this, and the longer we live the greater it should be. (Brigham Young, *JD* 14:229.)

The saving of souls takes more than experience. "It requires all the atonement of Christ, the mercy of the Father, the pity of angels and the grace of the Lord Jesus Christ to be with us always, and then to do the very best we possibly can, to get rid of this sin within us, so that we may escape from this world into the celestial kingdom" (Brigham Young, *JD* 11:301). Thus we must be prepared to be very patient while we work diligently, because we don't see our individual path ahead clearly.

We take as our model for sanctification the Lord Jesus Christ. The Apostle Peter testified: "God anointed Jesus of Nazareth with the Holy Ghost and with power: who went about doing good . . . for God was with him" (Acts 10:38). If we are going to take him as our model and go about doing good, we must first know what "good" is. Peter suggests that Jesus was able to do good because God was with him. Moroni gives us a further clarification of *good:* "And now I speak unto all the ends of the earth—that if the day cometh that the power and gifts of God shall be done away among you, it shall be because of *unbelief.* And wo be unto the children of men if this be the case; for there shall be none that doeth good among you, no not one. For if there be one among you that doeth good, he shall work by the power and gifts of God." (Moroni 10:24–25; emphasis added.) Moroni speaks of unbelief, which, of course, is a self-imposed limitation.

To do good, then, is to work by the gift and power of God. I think we may assume this definition of *good* wherever we find it in scripture. To do good we must seek to work by this gift. In that context let us consider first the inward preparation for sanctification and for doing good the Lord's way; and then the outward reach, or the power to draw others to the Lord Jesus Christ.

We are designed to increase (see Abraham 3:24–26), to be "added upon" with light, life, and glory, to exercise divine attributes and god-like powers. Joseph Smith enlightened us with this profound comment:

> We consider that God has created man with a mind capable of instruction, and a faculty which may be enlarged in proportion to the heed and diligence given to the light communicated from heaven to the intellect; and that the nearer man approaches perfection, the clearer are his views, and the greater his enjoyments, till he has overcome the evils of his life and lost every desire for sin; and like the ancients, arrives at that point of faith where he is wrapped in the power and glory of his Maker, and is caught up to dwell with Him. But we consider that this is a station to which no man ever arrived in a moment. He must have been instructed in the government and laws of that kingdom by proper degrees. (*TPJS*, p. 51.)

We must know and apply principles of truth in order to move along the path to godliness. Brigham Young spoke further on this godly increase:

> I have often told you from this stand, if you cleave to holy, godlike principles, you add more good to your organization . . . and the good spirit and influence which come from the Father of lights, and from Jesus Christ, and from the holy angels add good to it. . . . After a while the Lord will say . . . , "My son, you have been faithful, you have clung to good, and you love righteousness, and hate iniquity, from which you have turned away, now you shall have the blessing of the Holy Spirit to lead you, and be your constant companion, from this time henceforth and forever." Then the Holy Spirit becomes your property, it is given to you for a profit, and an eternal blessing. It tends to addition, extension, and increase, to immortality and eternal lives. (*JD* 2:135.)

Cleaving to holy principles adds power and light to our organization. *Cleave* suggests clinging to something without interruption. President Young obviously has reference to increasing in the Holy Ghost. We want this gift to increase in us until we are like the Lord himself, about whom John the Baptist remarked, "For God giveth him not the Spirit by measure, for he dwelleth in him, even the fulness" (John 3:34). This is the thing we want; we want to fulfill the law to that degree, to arrive at that point of fulness. This constant companionship of the Holy Ghost is a significant point in the process of being born again and that of being sanctified. Alma suggests that being born again is to be filled with the Holy Ghost: "I have labored without ceasing, that I might bring souls unto repentance; that I might bring them to taste of the exceeding joy of which I did taste; that they might also be born of God, and be filled with the Holy Ghost" (Alma 36:24).

Notice that Alma's focus is on bringing souls to Christ so that they can taste the joy he has tasted. This pursuit is the central thrust of his life. An important element of sanctification—maybe the critical element—is the desire to bring others to Christ and to want to give oneself to that above all other pursuits. So what is the process that brings us to that point of fulness, and how much can it be expedited? James E. Talmage said: "Somehow the Latter-day Saints have the mistaken notion that in the end, when the day comes that the Lord will make them gods or goddesses, when someone lays their hands on their heads and, as it were, says to them, You have now all that you need to be a God—go ahead—this is not true. All that you need to be a God is in you right now. Your job is to take those crude elements within you and refine them." (Quoted in Gene R. Cook, *Living by the Power of Faith* [Salt Lake City: Deseret Book, 1985], p. 91.) We may have been waiting for God to do something, but now it appears that he is waiting for us to do something.

The thing that we must do to be filled with the Holy Ghost brings us to what might be termed the power point—that pivotal point of having fulfilled a condition to get a blessing. We have to fulfill some kind of law (see D&C 130:20–21). The scriptures repeatedly describe this power point, that point at

which the blessing we want is released to us because we have
fulfilled the law. In the following short passages, notice words
like *all* and *every*.

— "It is by grace that we are saved, after all we can do" (2
    Nephi 25:23).
— "[The gifts of the Spirit] are given for the benefit of
    those who love me and keep all my commandments, and
    him that seeketh so to do" (D&C 46:9).
— "Bringing into captivity every thought to the obedience
    of Christ" (2 Corinthians 10:5).
— "Look unto me in every thought; doubt not, fear not"
    (D&C 6:36).
— "Cry unto God for all thy support; . . . let all thy doings
    be unto the Lord, and whithersoever thou goest let it be
    in the Lord; yea, let all thy thoughts be directed unto
    the Lord; . . . Counsel with the Lord in all thy doings . . .
    and if ye do these things, ye shall be lifted up at the last
    day." (Alma 37:36–37.)
— "Pray unto the Father with all the energy of heart, that
    ye may be filled with this love, which he hath bestowed
    upon all who are true followers of his Son, Jesus Christ;
    that ye may become the sons of God" (Moroni 7:48).

And so forth. The formula seems to be here, that when we
do all we can do toward the *all,* then the promise is released to
us. The power point is that point at which the intense desire of
our heart is fulfilled for us because we have done all we can do
to fulfill the law, not holding anything back from the Lord. For
example, it is when we move from sometimes-praying to nearly
all-times-praying that things change perceptibly. It is when
God's will becomes my will that power begins to break like the
sunlight in the morning, that the daystar arises in the heart, as
Peter wrote (see 2 Peter 1:19). The result is that one's access to
the Spirit becomes unrestricted; as President Young said, it has
become our property.

The Lord Jesus is our model for this principle of fully embracing the Father's will and thereby receiving power. It was by
this means that he was able to go about doing good. Abinadi
taught about the Savior's submission: "Yea, even so he shall be

led, crucified, and slain, the flesh becoming subject even unto death, the will of the Son being swallowed up in the will of the Father. And thus God breaketh the bands of death . . . giving the Son power to make intercession for the children of men." (Mosiah 15:7–8.) So we too, our wills swallowed up in the Savior's will, help to break the bands of our own spiritual death or separation from the Lord Jesus Christ.

During his mortal ministry the Lord said about himself: "I can of mine own self do nothing . . . I seek not mine own will, but the will of the Father which hath sent me" (John 5:30). "For I have not spoken of myself; but the Father which sent me, he gave me a commandment, what I should say, and what I should speak" (John 12:49). "The words that I speak unto you I speak not of myself; but the Father that dwelleth in me, he doeth the works" (John 14:10).

Just as the Father was the doer of all Jesus' deeds and the speaker of all his words, so the Lord Jesus offers the same essential relationship to each of us, and that relationship is indeed the only way to sanctification.

Let us observe that Jesus could not have been who he was had he not made his life all obedience, all prayer, all working by the gift and power of his Father. Although he had the same choice that you and I have to treat the Holy Ghost as optional, he chose to work only by the gift and power of God. He steadfastly cultivated the Spirit and learned to live in continual awareness of his Father's will as well as in possession of the power to do it. Herein were his perfection and sanctification.

Does this mean that you and I can't use our sense of humor? Or read a magazine? Or just let our minds relax? No, of course not. We're talking about establishing an inner environment, that submission to the Lord, in which everything else that lies in the full spectrum of wholesome human activity is done.

I think that inside each of us there smolders a desire to live and work by this power just as Jesus did—a divine urge coupled with a thrilling feeling of who we are and who we might become. Through the powers of the mind we can blow on those coals until the flame becomes intense and fulfills the law guarding the blessing. But how do we get from where we are now to that state of "all" by which the door to the treasure house of spiritual blessing swings open wide?

First, two things are essential for spiritual progress. For Latter-day Saints these two things seem commonplace by reason of counsel we constantly receive from our leaders, yet not all Saints comply. To those seeking sanctification, however, daily scripture study and "hearts drawn out in prayer unto [God] continually" (Alma 34:27) are crucial.

If we are hoping to do good the Lord's way, we must write the word of God on our hearts; we must obtain the word by feasting on scripture every day. As President Howard W. Hunter said, "The important thing is to allow nothing else to ever interfere with our study" (*Ensign*, November 1979, p. 64). Here, especially if we have little children or some other great demand on our time, we can only do the best we can, realizing that a very small amount, focused on, can be of great value, especially if it is held in the mind. But clearly, the greater the amount, the greater the blessing. "Seek not to declare my word, but first seek to obtain my word, and then shall your tongue be loosed; then, if you desire, you shall have my Spirit and my word, yea, the power of God unto the convincing of men" (D&C 11:21; see also Alma 17:2).

Formal and informal prayer, offered in the spirit of Moroni 10:4–5, must include a sincere heart, real intent, having faith in Christ; otherwise the prayers apparently do not set anything divine into motion. Without prayer we are just participating in man's righteousness, not God's (see Romans 10:2–3).

With scripture study and prayer as foundation, we are ready to consolidate our efforts to greater effect on the third issue. This point could be made in so many different ways that I've struggled to know how to say it succinctly, but it has to do with focusing our unfocused minds. Moroni gives the essential idea. You'll notice the word *all* coupled with the word *then:*

> Yea, come unto Christ, and be perfected in him, and deny yourselves of all ungodliness: and if ye shall . . . love God with all your might, mind, and strength, then is his grace sufficient for you, that by his grace ye may be perfect

in Christ; and if by the grace of God ye are perfect in Christ, ye can in nowise deny the power of God (Moroni 10:32).

The idea I want to concentrate on here is that the mind, informed by scripture and prayer and obedience, is the key to the treasures of faith, power in the Spirit, and sanctification. We do have the power to deny ourselves of all ungodliness by taking thought, by focusing our minds, if at the same time we choose to love God with all our might and strength. The power is already in us to do these things, otherwise the command would not be there. The Lord teaches that by fully immersing the heart and mind in a true idea, being fully baptized mentally in spiritual ideas, we unlock the powers of even the least educated or most modest mind.

Each of us has the ability to work in different mental modes, either natural or spiritual. It is with the spiritual mind that we open access to unseen spiritual powers and fill up with that heavenly gift that works inner miracles and gives us something of value to offer to others. Orson Hyde counseled: "[The mind] is the agent of the Almighty clothed with mortal tabernacles, and we must learn to discipline it, and bring it to bear on one point, and not allow the Devil to interfere or confuse it, nor divert it from the great object we have in view" (*JD* 7:153). And Orson Pratt observed: "If a person trains his mind to walk in the Spirit, and brings his whole mind to bear upon its operations, and upon the principles of faith which are calculated to put him in possession of the power of God, how much greater will be his facilities for attaining knowledge than those which any natural man possesses" (*JD* 7:155–56).

The fact that spiritual realities are unseen by our finite eyes does not diminish their reality or their power. They are real indeed. Spiritual blessings are accessed by the spiritually focused mind. We plant in our hearts and minds the true seeds of what we want, and then with cultivation these do bear their fruit. Alma says in his great discourse on faith, "But if ye neglect the tree, and take no thought for its nourishment" (Alma 32:38) the seed will die. He goes on: "If ye will not nourish the word, looking forward with an eye of faith [spiritually informed imagination] to the fruit thereof, ye can never pluck of the fruit of the tree of life."

Then he speaks of our diligence, faith, patience, and then plucking this most precious fruit, sweet, white, pure; and "ye shall feast upon this fruit even until ye are filled, that ye hunger not, neither shall ye thirst. Then, my brethren, ye shall reap the rewards of your faith, and your diligence, and patience, and long-suffering, waiting for the tree to bring forth fruit unto you." (Alma 32:40–43.)

Nourishing the seed or the word is by and large a mental process—taking thought, holding in thought with faith the things desired. For example, what if we would like to work by the gift and power of God, to have the Spirit of the Lord to be with us always in our dealing with others? Here is a specific idea from Brigham Young on focusing the mind in faith to bring to pass that desired blessing. "The Elders of Israel, though the great majority of them are moral men, and as clear of spot and blemish as men well can be, live beneath their privilege; they live continually without enjoying the power of God. I want to see men and women breathe the Holy Ghost in every breath of their lives, living constantly in the light of God's countenance." (*JD* 9:288–89.)

In saying he wished to see the Latter-day Saints breathe in the Holy Ghost with every breath, was President Young suggesting that the Spirit is really a form of energy that can nourish us physically?

Are we to understand this breathing in of the Spirit literally? The scriptures associate breathing with spirit and life. We are told the Gods "breathed into Adam's nostrils the breath of life" (Abraham 5:7). The resurrected Savior breathed on his Apostles and said, "Receive ye the Holy Ghost" (John 20:22). What does breathing in the Spirit mean?

I don't know. But what if I didn't analyze it but just turned my mind to do it? What if I were to take thought many times a day to "breathe in the Holy Ghost" and saw myself living in the light of God's countenance; his face smiling at me as I consciously tried to receive his Spirit, his will, his nature?

With these kinds of thoughts and mental exercises, I might begin to look around me to see what else I could do to turn my mind wholly to the Lord. Maybe I could help myself by posting scriptures around, maybe even pictures. I could use beautiful music to influence my spiritual feelings. What effect would these kinds of things have on my sanctification process? I would, without doubt, enjoy greater spiritual blessings, making their reality felt.

The Spirit has many manifestations. It can come through the spoken word—the human voice; it can come through music; it can come from the living word of God on the printed page, or directly from that Spirit itself; it can come from spiritual imagination and memory; it is often felt in places of natural beauty. We can use all these avenues to strengthen its influence on us. Alma says that it is discernible, and that one can taste the light (see Alma 32:35). There is no such thing as immaterial spirit; spirit is matter and it is energy (see D&C 131:7–8). The Spirit is something; it is real.

Life, love, and light are all forms of energy that emanate from the presence of God and "quicken" or energize all things according to the desire and mental focus of those being acted on (see D&C 88:11–13). Thoughts about and desires for godliness seem to increase the spiritual energy. Having this knowledge, why would we allow or invite any other kind of influence to affect our minds and faith?

What if I used my agency, after I began restructuring my environment, deliberately to generate thoughts and words of love to those around me? What if I took time and thought to listen carefully to the people around me for their special messages? What if I took thought to cherish the people around me? I would cause delicate godly powers to gain strength. The Spirit would be attracted to these simple efforts. Would I not feel that the sanctification process was truly going forward?

What if I thought just about my voice for a moment, even my tone of voice? Nephi teaches about speaking with the gift and power of God—he calls it the tongue of angels, who speak by the Holy Ghost (2 Nephi 31:14; 32:2–3). What if we were to do what the Lord said to Joseph Smith and Sidney Rigdon?

"Lift up your voices unto this people; speak the thoughts that I shall put into your hearts. . . . For it shall be given you in the very hour, yea, in the very moment, what ye shall say. But a commandment I give unto you, that ye shall declare whatsoever thing ye declare in my name, in solemnity of heart, in the spirit of meekness, in all things. And I give unto you this promise, that inasmuch as ye do this the Holy Ghost shall be shed forth in bearing record unto all things whatsoever ye shall say." (D&C 100:5–8.)

Amulek told Zeezrom, "I shall say nothing which is contrary to the Spirit of the Lord" (Alma 11:22).

An additionally helpful measure might be to team up with someone else—a family member or a friend—who is interested in the same spiritual pursuits as you are, whom you can help and who can help you keep focused (see Mosiah 26:39; Colossians 3:16; Romans 15:14).

What if I just quit wasting time and decided to make every breath, every thought, every word, every act rooted somehow in my love for and conscious awareness of the Lord? But then the Lord has already asked us to do just that; therefore, we can exercise unlimited faith in these possibilities, knowing that the Lord will add his strengthening grace as we diligently bring our thoughts into subjection to him.

We might try an experiment: Think for a moment of the Lord Jesus Christ, your love for him, his love for you, your feelings of tenderness for him; perhaps a time when he blessed you and you knew it: *immediately* you have opened your access to the Spirit of the Lord. One can feel that feeling and enlarge on it. One could consciously take several deep breaths, breathing in the delicate, tender presence of the Spirit of the Lord. Now, let whatever one said or did be in the context of those thoughts and feelings. One would then be working by the gift and power of God at least in a small degree.

At first our power may be small, but as we practice, not requiring too much reward at first, we will feel the increasing reality of the Spirit. One might make an analogy with an old-fashioned iron pump: one pumps hard patiently; then a trickle comes, then a good stream, then a gush of water. We must develop the patience of Job with these spiritual processes. The Lord said so kindly: "Ye are not able to abide the presence of God now, neither the ministering of angels; wherefore, continue in patience until ye are perfected" (D&C 67:13).

Elder M. Russell Ballard said: "I understand the power and the reality of the Spirit of the Lord today in a way that I did not believe would ever be possible in my lifetime. . . . Learning to respond to the promptings of the Spirit did not all of a sudden happen in my life, but it has grown 'line upon line, precept upon precept, here a little and there a little'" (2 Nephi 28:30). ("Respond to the Prompting of the Spirit," Address to Religious Educators, 8 January 1988, p. 53.)

As we concentrate our efforts, little rewards do begin to appear and whet our thirst for more; we can feel that we are growing in the gift and power of God. The Spirit can't be forced—it is delicate; but we can apply principles and reap the blessings and learn to work in our little spheres as God works in his great one.

What kinds of changes could we make in a few days, or weeks, or months? We might be surprised as the Lord's power connects with ours.

The person who has put his or her mind consciously onto the sanctification path, who is striving to pray without ceasing in faith that one might really accomplish that, is undergoing wonderful changes. This person is in a continual state of renewal. Yesterday is gone, and who he was and what she was don't matter anymore. What matters is *now*, this present moment, and our quest that moves patiently forward. Our spiritual efforts are the preparation for everything required of us. How often we have dissipated our energies because we have not focused on getting the power of God to do them!

It is interesting that we can only work by the gift of God in the present moment. Living and working in the now, we will not dwell on past mistakes nor project worry into the future— these thoughts violate spiritual law. Focusing on now, bringing oneself from an out-of-focus condition into a single spiritual focus, reduces stress, because one is not trying to deal with so many things at once, especially painful things. Stuff piles up in the mind, and we need to rinse our minds clean of the things that bring pain to ourselves or others. The Lord said to Martha, who was troubled and anxious, "One thing is needful" (Luke 10:42). And he says to us, "Look unto me in every thought; doubt not, fear not" (D&C 6:36). It is for our blessing that the Lord asks us to make our eye single to his glory, for then "your whole bodies shall be filled with light, and there shall be no darkness in you; and that body which is filled with light comprehendeth all things. Therefore, sanctify yourselves that your minds become single to God, and the days will come that you shall see him." (D&C 88:67–68.)

Up to this point I have been discussing the sanctification of ourselves, out of the conviction that we help others best when we are working on our own sanctification. Thus we avoid the mote-beam problem (see 3 Nephi 14:3). Then we can sense better the possible impurity in our own motives—desires to control, to get vengeance, to manipulate or force something on those we love or want to love. We can receive by the Spirit unexpected directions to go—maybe even to do nothing for the time being—except work on ourselves.

Thus the Savior said on the eve of the greatest act of sanctification ever performed: "For their sakes, I sanctify myself" (John 17:19). His desire to sanctify himself rose out of his love. Ammon, one of the sons of Mosiah, showed a similar pattern: "He that repenteth and exerciseth faith, and bringeth forth good works, and prayeth continually without ceasing—unto such it is given to know the mysteries of God; yea, unto such it shall be given to reveal things which never have been revealed; yea, and it shall be given unto such to bring thousands of souls to repentance" (Alma 26:22; see also D&C 6:11).

We read many examples in scripture of those who sanctified their lives and then had a saving influence on others. For instance, the fathers Alma and Mosiah performed a redeeming function, praying for their wayward sons, which brought an angel who made a terrific impression on them. Alma the Younger fell into a comatose state. The priests then, standing in their redemptive roles, fasted and prayed two days and two nights in his behalf. He stood up before them and recounted the miracle of his rebirth. (See Mosiah 27.) Our secret, vibrant, love-filled prayers for someone else are a pure form of love, and they really matter.

Elder Cook made the observation that through prayer we can assist others in reaching the point of "all." He said with respect to assisting a person who was trying to fulfill his part in working on a problem spiritually: "There is power in uniting in prayer on something, and the additional prayers of people . . . help you put in what is required more quickly so you can reach the point where you have truly done all in your part. And when you have, then the Lord can act and will by law." ("Teaching by the Spirit and Learning How to Receive Blessings from the Lord," CES Seminary and Institute Meeting, 30 June 1989.)

In general conference 1992 Elder Boyd K. Packer quoted Elder Orson F. Whitney, who was quoting Joseph Smith: "The Prophet Joseph Smith declared—and he never taught a more comforting doctrine—that the eternal sealings of faithful parents and the divine promises made to them for valiant service in the Cause of Truth, would save not only themselves, but likewise their posterity. . . . Pray for your careless and disobedient children; hold on to them with your faith. Hope on, trust on, till you see the salvation of God." (Orson F. Whitney, in Conference Report, April 1929, p. 110.)

These are promises made to members who diligently seek their sanctification. I do not know how this principle works, but I think we may safely assume that our efforts at sanctification can work forwards and backwards and sideways, on all our loved ones.

Many of the people around us are hungry for spiritual things. When we take thought to work by the gift and power of God we find that we are piercing the veil. We come to sense needs in others and often find we have the blessing they need. We learn that by simply seeking to work by the gift and power of God, by taking thought, we become carriers of the Spirit. In this context we know that we are truly nothing; it is the Spirit acting through us that blesses.

Like the Savior, one who consciously carries the Spirit can change some things forever. Think about what we could do for troubled family members through fasting, prayer, and spiritual focus, or for our visiting teaching sisters, or whoever we found that the Lord was drawing us to. James wrote, "The effectual fervent prayer of a righteous man availeth much" (James 5:16).

Because we are fallen, and suffering somewhat in that condition, we will sometimes feel the apparent hopelessness of our own quest for sanctification—it will seem too hard. That is the moment when we begin to understand what Jesus Christ is offering. He seems to respond more than anything to our desires to love and bless. We must press forward with a steadfastness in Christ (see 2 Nephi 31:20), no matter what, just as the brother of Jared did, who lamented over his fallen condition just in the moments before the Lord took him through the cloud-veil into His presence: "Because of the fall our natures have become evil continually; nevertheless, O Lord, thou hast given us a commandment that we must call upon thee, that from thee we may receive according to our desires" (Ether 3:2).

We remember the Lord's counsel:

> Pray always, and I will pour out my Spirit upon you, and great shall be your blessing. . . .
>
> Behold, canst thou [hear] this without rejoicing and lifting up thy heart for gladness?
>
> Or canst thou run about longer as a blind guide?
>
> Or canst thou be humble and meek, and conduct thyself wisely before me? Yea, come unto me thy Savior. (D&C 19:38–41.)

CHAPTER TEN

❧

Spiritual Discouragement

In this chapter I am talking not about the spiritual discouragement that comes from overt sinning but the kind that comes to the person who is aspiring to be a true disciple of the Lord Jesus Christ. There is a crucial secret kept from the natural man that the aspiring disciple begins to learn early on; that is, that he is fallen, he is lost, and was born into spiritual death (see Helaman 14:16). The truth of one's real condition, of one's deeply fallen and lost state, is slowly unveiled to the person who is trying to become a true disciple. As the veil lifts a little more and a little more, we, like the people of King Benjamin, view ourselves in our carnal state; or like the brother of Jared at the cloud-veil, we see that our natures "have become evil continually" (Ether 3:2).

As our discipleship to the Lord Jesus Christ deepens and our true condition becomes more apparent to us, our susceptibility to a particular kind of discouragement may increase. The true disciple may be, in some ways, more subject to crushing feelings of discouragement and worthlessness than the natural man is. It may be that the harder the aspiring true disciple tries, the more discouraged he or she will become. Yet each of us knows that we cannot stop trying with all our might, mind, and strength, even while we feel so inadequate.

With respect to man's fallen condition, Brigham Young said: "We know the design of our Father in heaven in creating the earth and in peopling it, and bringing forth the myriads of organizations which dwell upon it. We know that all this is for his glory—to swell the eternities that are before him with intelligent beings who are capable of enjoying the height of glory. But, before we can come in possession of this, we need large experience, and its acquisition is a slow process. Our lives here are for the purpose of acquiring this, and the longer we live the greater it should be." (*JD* 14:229.)

How patient we have to be at the slowness of our progress! The making of mistakes and the failing to measure up just seem to be beyond our ability to avoid. And the hardest thing about many of our mistakes is that they happen when we are trying our very best to do well the things that matter the very most: our family relationships, our other relationships, our Church work, our jobs, our schoolwork.

Maybe the hardest part of earth life for spiritually sensitive people is their very imperfection. Joseph F. Smith wrote: "I think that the spirit, before and after this probation, possesses greater facilities, aye, manifold greater, for the acquisition of knowledge, than while manacled and shut up in the prison-house of mortality" (*Gospel Doctrine*, p. 13).

This fallen condition requires more humility and patience than we normally want to exercise. Nevertheless, our imperfection is left pretty firmly in place while we are here on earth.

In addition, along the way, the Lord chastens us from time to time because he loves us; a little experience comes to us like a spur and brings us up short, and we realize that there are changes we must make. And that spur can feel like pretty tough love. But of course it's all part of the process of discipleship.

Not only our fallenness causes us trouble, but Satan too

gets involved. He and his cohorts are always combing the earth for people to trouble. He finds a good Latter-day Saint who is giving his or her all. Satan's name in Greek is *dia'bolos,* which means "hurler of accusations." He hurls accusations at us and gets us to beat on ourselves. He stirs around in our miserable feelings and seeks to shut us right down—that is, if we can get discouraged enough, if we just stop trying, if we come to a dead standstill on the path up Mount Sinai and say, "I've had enough," and turn around and start back down again. We don't even have to commit any big sins—he has us where he wants us.

Part of enduring to the end may have to do with just keeping on trying *against* feelings of overwhelming inadequacy—knowing they are part of discipleship, but knowing too that we must keep on going as best we can, no matter how bad we feel!

A person may think that his feelings of hopelessness reflect his true condition, but they do not. These feelings are a smoke screen, or maybe mists of darkness, generated by a true sense of one's fallenness—but with which Satan has connected, instead of the Savior. Satan is a secondary infection; just as in the case of the bacteria that grows in us as we're getting sick, we may not really feel the infection come, and we do not for a while discern its nature. Then one day the light suddenly goes on and we realize that Satan is trying to shut us down; then we can, with our faith in the Lord Jesus Christ, kick him out—for a while, at least.

Nephi cried out, "O wretched man that I am! Yea, my heart sorroweth because of my flesh; my soul grieveth because of mine iniquities. I am encompassed about, because of the temptations and the sins which do so easily beset me." (2 Nephi 4:17–18.)

In the middle of that psalm, apparently, Nephi figured out that Satan, the enemy of his soul, was making trouble for him. He said: "Yea, why should I give way to temptations, that the evil one have place in my heart to destroy my peace and afflict my soul?. . . Awake, my soul! No longer droop in sin. Rejoice, O my heart, and give place no more for the enemy of my soul." (2 Nephi 4:27–28.)

It helps me to know that the greatest spirits among us fight discouragement—today, right now. We could produce many case studies.

I had the privilege of listening to one of the Brethren describe the crushing feelings of incapacity he had upon his call to his high position in the Church. It was very moving to hear him describe his distress. It was also, at the same time, strangely reassuring. Not only did I see my own discouragement in a new light, but also I made the commitment to pray more fervently for the Brethren. I realized that they really need our prayers.

Elder Spencer W. Kimball is an example of one who never seemed to feel adequate in his calling, at least in the early days of his apostleship. He seemed always to feel that he wasn't measuring up. Here is his description of his first experience sitting with the Brethren on the stand at general conference:

"How weak I felt! How humble I was! How grateful I was when President McKay said the voting was unanimous. I seemed to be swimming in a daze. It seemed so unreal and impossible that I—just poor weak Spencer Kimball—could be being sustained as an Apostle of the Lord Jesus Christ, and tears welled in my eyes again as I heard myself sustained as an Apostle, a prophet, seer and revelator to the Church. We were called to the stand and took our places with the Twelve Apostles. I was next to Brother Lee who squeezed my arm in welcome. Thousands of eyes were upon us appraising, weighing, honoring us. . . . After some other talks I was called on for my maiden talk. How I reached the pulpit I hardly know. What a moment—a sea of upturned, wondering, expectant faces met my first gaze. I began. . . . I must have taken about 15 minutes. I lost track of time as I poured out my appreciation and gratitude and bore testimony.

"As I took my seat I felt I had failed and continued to tell myself that I had failed as Brother Benson gave his simple sweet-spirited testimony."

The next day Spencer and Ezra Taft Benson waited upon President Grant in the big room next to the President's office. . . . Spencer Kimball knelt at the feet of the invalid Prophet, who had been born before the Civil War and who now laid his hands on his head, joined by the other Apostles, and ordained Spencer Woolley Kimball an Apostle. "What rapture—What bliss and joy unspeakable!"

But not long after, in his journal one day he wrote:

"I have been depressed all day—I feel so inadequate. It seems that I am not succeeding with my work as I should like. It has been a hectic day. Everything seems to have been disturbing and disappointing. Received a long letter of severe criticism from one of my friends—and everything seemed to be at cross-purposes. Maybe I needed further humbling."

Then he wrote four days later:

"Oh! I am so happy today. To see just a little fruit of our labors is encouraging." (Edward L. Kimball and Andrew E. Kimball, Jr., *Spencer W. Kimball* [Salt Lake City: Bookcraft, 1977], pp. 204–5, 210–11.)

Clearly discouragement is the means by which Satan tries to get us to stop trying. He knows that if we keep trying we're going to connect with the Spirit of the Lord, which takes us out of our narrow self-preoccupation and unveils a rich resource of power and capacity.

It seems to me that our reaction to our heightened feelings of fallenness is important. One thing that seems to help is humility. It is a paradox that, when we feel so everlastingly valueless, the thing that could bring relief is humility. But discouragement may reveal a weakened connection with the Savior, a blurred focus. We can sharpen our focus by humbling ourselves to the depths before him. Then he offers us a sip out of the cup of his Spirit and our perspective changes, and we know that in his strength we can go on and even feel a measure of success. We can appreciate Ammon's words: "Yea, I know that I am nothing; as to my strength I am weak; therefore I will not boast of myself, but I will boast of my God, for in his strength I can do all things" (Alma 26:12).

Another helpful thing is the realization that we are all in this together. Whether my spiritually striving neighbor shows it or not, he or she is suffering from the same growing pains I am. Just knowing that many faces I meet have these sensitive feelings behind them helps me know how to treat others better and at the same time seems to heal me too.

A third thing that helps is suggested by the Apostle John:

> My little children, let us not love in word, neither in tongue; but in deed and in truth.
>
> And hereby we know that we are of the truth, and shall assure our hearts before him.
>
> For if our heart condemn us, God is greater than our heart, and knoweth all things.
>
> Beloved, if our heart condemn us not, then have we confidence toward God.
>
> And whatsoever we ask, we receive of him, because we keep his commandments, and do those things that are pleasing in his sight.
>
> And this is his commandment, That we should believe on the name of his Son Jesus Christ, and love one another, as he gave us commandment.
>
> And he that keepeth his commandments dwelleth in him, and he in him. And hereby we know that he abideth in us, by the Spirit which he hath given us. (1 John 3:18–24.)

This passage says to me that even though our hearts condemn us, we can know that, if we are growing in the commandment to love, our hearts can be assured before him; he will dwell in us and we in him.

Our fallenness is, in itself, not a state of guilt, but it makes us highly vulnerable to guilt and self-doubt. Of course, the depth of our self-doubt is the beginning of the measure of our need for the Lord Jesus Christ. Ultimately our woeful feelings will be displaced forever with his sublime love. Until then we must press on.

President Howard Hunter spoke about the apostolic calling and illustrated the model for us:

> As special witnesses of our Savior, we have been given the awesome assignment to administer the affairs of his church and kingdom and to minister to his daughters and his sons wherever they are on the face of the earth. By reason of our call to testify, govern, and minister, it is required of us that despite age, infirmity, exhaustion, and feelings of inadequacy, we do the work he has given us to do, to the last breath of our lives. ("To the Women of the Church," *Ensign,* November 1992, p. 96.)

May we stretch beyond our painful inadequacy and press on in the Lord's strength.

CHAPTER ELEVEN

Healing Through Repentance

Being at least a little neurotic myself as an adult child of an alcoholic father, I have sought healing from emotional confusions and troubles. And as a teacher of young adults, I have seen a number of young people from troubled families in the Church; people from homes in which there is alcoholism, sexual abuse, workaholism, too much anger, emotional neglect, obsession with image—especially of the smooth, glossy LDS family on the outside but hiding the grieving and troubled family inside. What does God offer to these people?

Truly, many of us have been wounded. Some have received very grievous wounds, in some cases from the very people they should have been able to trust for help. This is a terrible but common paradox. By the abundance of wounds around us, it would seem that a major function of this earth life is to teach us what to do about wounds.

On our part we just want to come to God and receive rapid healing; but on his part he sees that there are some things we have to understand first, some things *we* have to do. We're here on earth to learn about human/divine dynamics, how people prosper and the principles upon which God prospers them. He often requires our participation in our own healing because he is bent on a much grander transformation than just the remedy for one particular situation. There is always more than one thing that needs healing or changing in our lives. Healing may involve fundamental changes; therefore, healing is a process by which things usually get better little by little. Elder Richard G. Scott remarked: "Understand that healing can take considerable time. Recovery generally comes in steps. It is accelerated when gratitude is expressed to the Lord for every degree of improvement noted." ("Healing the Tragic Scars of Abuse," *Ensign*, May 1992, p. 32.)

One might well ask how there can be a benevolent purpose in a wound-inflicting world. We remember that one purpose of this life is to prepare to meet God (see Alma 34:32); in particular, as Paul taught, we are, by our experiences here, "to be conformed to the image of [Christ]" (Romans 8:29). It would seem, then, that only in a pain-inflicting world can we be conformed to the image of Christ. Christ himself came into a cruel world to the only people who would have crucified him (see 2 Nephi 10:3).

Joseph Smith's salvation was hammered out in a similar way. In Liberty Jail, writing to a friend who had tried to visit him but was prevented by the guards, but whom he could see through the bars, he said:

I was glad to see you. No tongue can tell what inexpressible joy it gives a man, after having been enclosed in the walls of a prison for five months, to see the face of one who has been a friend. It seems to me that my heart will always be more tender after this than ever it was before. . . . For my part, I think I never could have felt as I now do, if I had not suffered the wrongs that I have suffered. All things shall work together for good to them that love God. . . . Do not have any feelings of enmity towards any son or daughter of Adam. . . . We must not take it in our hands to avenge our wrongs. Vengeance is mine, saith the Lord, and I will repay. (*History of the Church* 3:285–86.)

The function of wounds is to tenderize our souls, again to conform us to the image of Christ.

On the necessity of being tried by pain, President John Taylor told the Saints, quoting Joseph Smith: "You will have all kinds of trials to pass through. And it is quite as necessary that you be tried as it was for Abraham and other men of God. . . . God will feel after you, and he will take hold of you and wrench your very heart strings, and if you cannot stand it you will not be fit for an inheritance in the Celestial Kingdom of God." (*JD* 24:197.)

We must beware because, though our trials may have been given us for benevolent purposes, if we are not careful we can interpret them the wrong way and become bitter and despondent, thereby cutting ourselves off from the most potent sources of healing. Sometimes our greatest trials come from our misguided reactions to some initial pain.

To examine these ideas more closely I want to give a particular example of a family whose hearts' strings were wrenched. This family had an alcoholic father. The atmosphere was tense, full of conflict; the parents were distracted and preoccupied with their own problems and, as a result, their child was not nurtured in any consistent way. Emptiness, insecurity, pain became the child's frequent companions, although she did not sense them consciously. She couldn't express her feelings to her parents because she sensed that they couldn't cope with the guilt of her emotional problems. Parent reacted against parent in manipulative ways, teaching the child principles of unstable relationships, violations of the laws of love, of God's laws. The child hurt; the parents hurt, because, in all likelihood, their parents before them hurt too.

The child's troubles do not magically disappear as the child becomes an adult. Most children carry the family's sins into the next generation. Therefore the chain is not broken, generation after generation, so long as the children mimic the dynamics of their childhood families. What is the solution? Someone must break the chain of pain. The sinned-against child must seek healing and cease to sin.

Children come out of such families with many distorted feelings about how people relate to each other. They have trouble in identifying their real feelings. Often they are perfectionistic and subject to depression, self-critical, driven and tense, angry, guilty, preoccupied with need for approval from others. When they become parents they are irritable with their young families and often make trouble in their families. They feel they are barely able to keep their resentment from seeping out. True, they were sinned against, but, more important, they are also sinning. One of the most powerful keys to getting well is to accept that the sinned-against person must repent of his or her sins, which actually cause much more trouble than the sins committed against them.

The man or woman who was sinned against may victimize others in overt or subtle ways. It is important to point out that, so preoccupied is she with her own pain, that she may not see consciously that she is doing anything wrong at all. She is in a survival mode, a self-preservation mode. She can only blame others. But her unconscious, her spirit, knows that she is sinning against the light and against herself. Aware or not, she is the victim of the laws she is violating, and only the truth and her repentance will make healing possible.

Specifically, her self-preoccupation, her stress, her manipulation and control of others, her perfectionism, her hysteria, her emotional dishonesty, her leaking resentment, her blaming of others, her self-pity, her moodiness, her defensiveness—all these behaviors do two things: first, they burden her own sensitive soul with layers of painful remorse and guilt; then, her abuse of those around her adds to her burden, the law of restoration working against her and returning into her own soul the distress she has caused. The key point here is that *the sin we do now is more destructive to us than the sin done against us.* The love we are not giving now causes us more trouble than the love that was not given to us. The wounds we give others wound our own souls.

The victim may have become the victimizer. No matter how justified she is in having developed these behaviors, she can't be healed until she begins to give them up. She thinks that her distress comes from the wounds inflicted on her; and of course those wounds are real. But her greatest distress may come from the way she has continued to respond to her wounds. Here is the spiritual principle: "Wickedness never was happiness. . . . For that which ye do send out shall return unto you again, and be restored." (Alma 41:10, 15.)

The startling insight in these situations is that most of one's distress is self-inflicted—a thought that might make one angry if revealed at the wrong moment. The last thing a hurting person wants to hear is the fact that if she is in emotional hell, she in some way helped both to create it and perpetuate it.

Of course the liberating truth is that one's hell can be uncreated, but, oh, how much humility the uncreation takes! One feels humiliation as she realizes how much hurt she has unnecessarily inflicted on herself and her loved ones. We are so late smart. By the time we get smart, we have to live with the consequences of the un-smart things we did. It helps to laugh about it. And we can finally laugh about it, because through the power of the Atonement, nothing we have done is beyond repair.

One important insight along the way for the healing person is that in her own mind she has not classified her trouble-causing behavior as sin. There are the large, obvious sins like murder and adultery—these may or may not have been at issue. We would expect to suffer for those. But in reality it is also the so-called "small sins" that cause much trouble. Often one does not see one's faulty thinking and behavior as sins, but in that they are violations of love, and in that they constitute abuse for oneself and others, one has to admit that they are indeed sins. It is a revelation to realize that the principles of Jesus Christ are designed to trim away the very behaviors that cause one the most trouble and to impart that peace "which passeth all understanding" (Philippians 4:7).

Much peace comes with relaxing our grip on our resentment against our abusers and ceasing to give our own wounds too much power. We can decide to reserve judgment about the ones who abused us and look forward to the day when we are able to drop all charges against them. We can, in addition, finally give up trying to get compensation for what happened to us in the past. These are things we are able to do as the healing process gets under way. Forgiveness may be defined as "the choice to no longer allow the memory of the abuse to continue to abuse." (Marie Fortune, "Forgiveness: The Last Step," in *Abuse and Religion*, ed. Anne L. Horton [Lexington, Massachusetts: D.C. Heath and Co., 1988], p. 218.)

We can change many of our behaviors, but we know that that is not enough. How do we change feelings? Here the Atonement's power is so precious. I can remember one particular painful visit back to my childhood home a few years ago. I had by that time received a good deal of healing from the combination of the Lord's help and from Al-Anon. But upon crossing the threshold of my childhood home, somehow I got hooked right back into my family's old troubles. Many abusive accusations were hurled, much bitterness was vented, many hot tears were shed. Afterwards, returning to my present home emotionally dazed, I did not think I could ever recover from such pain, from such intense self-anger over having gotten hooked once again into the family neurosis, especially since I thought we were all doing so much better. Weeks went by, and months. I couldn't think of the experience with anything but grief and, worst of all, a feeling of God's having betrayed me.

Then one day, while I was reading the scriptures, I realized that something had just neutralized my heart's pain over that dreadful experience. The pain was absolutely gone. In its place was compassion for myself and for all the participants in that awful confrontation. I knew that God had just sent his grace into my heart. I was healed of that experience.

The dynamics of healing defy analysis, but clearly to get something we must seek it—by praying intensively, reading, talking. Sometimes, instead of seeking the help we need, we actually resist what the Lord is trying to do for us. Sometimes we may fool ourselves and only seem to be seeking help—we read book after book, we talk, we mentally churn, we discuss, but we don't *change ourselves*. We may be "ever learning, and never able to come to the knowledge of the truth" (2 Timothy 3:7).

The answers to our questions may have presented themselves to us again and again. But we may cling to our comfortable old hurts and abuses, finding some kind of perverse pleasure in them. Healing begins with the desire to be healed and to be changed (Alma 32:27). It is interesting that before he healed them the Savior often asked people if they wanted to be healed.

The Lord speaks of the conditions for healing: "After their temptations, and much tribulation, behold, I, the Lord, will feel after them, and if they harden not their hearts, and stiffen not their necks against me, they shall be converted, and I will heal them" (D&C 112:13).

When we fully see the real sin (as opposed to the false guilt we may have carried) in our own hearts, we might cry out as the Lamanite king did to Aaron: "What shall I do that I may be born of God, having this wicked spirit rooted out of my breast, and receive his Spirit, that I may be filled with joy?" (Alma 22:15.) Aaron instructed him to bow down and pray, upon which he prayed, "O God, Aaron hath told me that there is a God; and if there is a God, and if thou art God, wilt thou make thyself known unto me, and I will give away all my sins to know thee" (Alma 22:18). One might notice that healing comes from changing oneself rather than another person.

I think suffering is necessary in this life, but it is not necessary to continue to suffer. Life does not need to be defined by suffering. I've decided, in fact, that God designed a glory to come out of a person's sufferings. A person can foil her wounds' negative power by making a decision to use them, not as an excuse to be miserable and to inflict misery on others, but to turn the energy of her suffering and compassion to divine purposes. She can use her suffering to be conformed to the image of Jesus Christ. She can triumph over her sorrow by offering deep tenderness and kindness to relieve suffering among her loved ones and others. Elder Marvin J. Ashton said, "When the virtue of charity becomes implanted in your heart, you are never the same again. It makes the thought of being a basher repulsive." ("The Tongue Can Be a Sharp Sword," *Ensign*, May 1992, p. 19.)

There are no solutions to our problems that are not finally

spiritual and follow the highly therapeutic information scattered throughout the scriptures. We have esteemed it too lightly (D&C 84:54–57). Deep spiritual therapy cannot be approached casually, but the principles are really simple: we come to God with all the energy of heart that we can bring, all the careful obedience that we can muster, and he comes to us, step by step, closer and closer until the perfect day (D&C 50:24).

Can everything be "faithed away"? That is, if we have sufficient faith, can anything we want be healed? Apparently not, because faith is not the only variable in healing. In the Apostle Paul's case, for example, describing an infirmity in his flesh which he calls a thorn, he writes: "For this thing I besought the Lord thrice, that it might depart from me. And he [the Lord] said unto me, My grace is sufficient for thee: for my strength is made perfect in weakness" (2 Corinthians 12:8–9). Some infirmities will remain, not from lack of faith or lack of worthiness but according to the Lord's wisdom. Therefore, we learn to exercise faith, not in the thing we think we have to have, but in the Lord Jesus Christ and his plan for us, whatever that is. I learned (imperfectly) to live the Al-Anon Serenity Prayer: "God grant me the serenity to accept the things I cannot change, courage to change the things I can, and wisdom to know the difference."

What each of us needs, no matter what the wounds in our lives, is to be reborn and simply to come to Christ with no reservations. We want to learn frequent, focused, fervent prayer and to live deliberately and spiritually—not according to the precepts of men. Simply, a work needs to be done in us that only Christ can do.

One day the Jews will confront their Messiah and ask him what the wounds are in his hands and feet. He will answer poignantly, "These wounds are the wounds with which I was wounded in the house of my friends" (D&C 45:52). Here is that terrible paradox again of betrayal by those who should have been the nurturers. But the Lord Jesus Christ shows us that there is a triumph, a glory, designed to come out of wounds.

CHAPTER TWELVE

Agents of Healing

I tried to write about one group of people here, namely, the growing numbers of the sinned-against among us. But I couldn't keep the young sinner out of this discussion because he or she is so often the same person. My remarks are directed to Church teachers and leaders.

In our efforts to make sin seem despicable to the people in our classes, we may make *them* feel despicable. We have, for example, heard of teaching chastity by passing a fresh rose through eight or so young hands during a chastity lesson; the rose ends up looking pretty bedraggled and is, unfortunately, equated with the unchaste young person. I'm worried about two people who may be sitting in the class during such a lesson: 1) the girl or boy who has actually been unchaste, and 2) the girl or boy who has been abused but had no power to stop the abuse and feels permanently damaged and unclean.

If you have taught such a lesson, do not be dismayed. You are not alone, and it may have been entirely appropriate under the circumstances. But increasingly our classes have children who come from troubled families, youth who have had more sexual experience than perhaps any generation that has sat in our classes heretofore. These abused children and young sinners appear in even our best families; when they appear the Lord can teach the parents, who are often the Church leaders, how to deepen their spirituality and their love, and how to fight more effectively the battle that is raging out there for the souls of our children. It seems that the Lord is preparing an increasing number of Saints to act as agents of healing. We well know that those who have felt the sorrow of abuse in their midst can be especially tender and inspired healers. Thus, many of us suffer in order to pass on the healing.

In our families we must set aside our personal fear, even feelings of humiliation or invalidation as parents, and just learn all we can about the dynamics of healing from abuse. Sometimes a parent's most painful response to a revelation of his or her child's abuse is guilt—real or false. How important it is to set aside pride, to let go of false guilt and unearned humiliation; or to repent as necessary, so that the way is cleared to give real, untainted love and support to the abused one. (See Alma 7:11–12 for the point that the Savior suffered so that he could heal us. Many of us follow in his pattern.)

Our attitudes toward sinners or the sinned-against are very important as we try to save the children. I feel deeply that the fostering of self-loathing in our classes is contrary to the mission of the Lord Jesus Christ. Our prayerful concern must be that, as we teach, our words *draw* the offended, as well as the guilty, to the arms of the Savior, and not cause them to flee, fearful of the self-loathing that they may feel most intensely within the walls of our church houses. Some suggestions for teaching follow:

With respect to teaching faith in God, we need to know that sometimes the offended child prayed to the Lord to be protected from the abuse, but deliverance did not come when it was asked for. An urgent question may be, not only for the sinned-against but also for his or her loved ones, "Why didn't God protect me?" "How can I pray to a God that I cannot trust?" "How can I live with confidence in such a dangerous world where anything can happen to me?" Many children have been taught that if they pray hard enough and are good enough, God will protect them. Then something happens from which they were not protected. How is their faith restored?

There seem to be stages in healing and restoration of trust. The Apostle Paul speaks of that peace which passes all understanding (see Philippians 4:7) suggesting that there is a peace available that bypasses the cognitive processes of the mind. In the very beginning of healing, no adequate words can explain the abuse because the offended one's grief and sense of loss are so great that the mind cannot accommodate a rational answer. The path to healing at this point may lie not so much in words of explanation as in *feeling*, because the greatest damage lies in the offended one's feelings. The greatest need, therefore, lies in the feelings and may be twofold: to get the poisonous, toxic feelings about the abuse out—by crying, by screaming, by very angry expressions, by hashing and rehashing the abuse. These must be allowed for a time. But one must take care not to get stuck in these feelings. Elder Richard G. Scott gives helpful advice on the therapeutic process by pointing out that any therapy that "engenders hatred, despondency, distrust, anger, or revenge must be supplanted by the tender mercies of a loving Father in Heaven and His Beloved Son. When anguish comes from evil acts of others, there should be punishment and corrective action taken, but the offended is not the one to initiate that action. Leave it to others who have that responsibility. Learn to forgive; though terribly hard, it will release you and open the way to a newness of life." ("To Be Healed," *Ensign*, May 1994, p. 9.)

The second great need is to take good feeling in—to feel full support, love, protection, and reassurance that getting help was the right thing to do—no matter what the consequences of the revelation of abuse may have been. Often the sinned-against have been made to feel responsible for the abuse. They must be reassured that they are not guilty.

Often they feel that they are intrinsically bad because God protects some people but did not protect them, or that no one would do these things to them if they did not deserve them. Might it help to remind them of the innocent suffering of the Prophet Joseph who prayed, "O God, where art thou?" (D&C 121:1) or of the Savior himself who cried out, "My God, my God, why hast thou forsaken me?" (Matthew 27:46)? Let the children know that they are among the most precious spirits that God ever had in his heaven, and that they were called and foreordained in heaven to be exalted in due time. The Apostle Paul teaches about the blessing of this premortal calling and the purpose of earth's experiences: "And we know that all things work together for good to them that love God, to them who are the called according to his purpose. For whom he did foreknow, he also did predestinate [foreordain] to be conformed to the image of his Son" (Romans 8:28–29). Teach them that we can become great, not in spite of our innocent suffering but *because* of it.

But satisfying verbal answers to life's terrible questions do not readily present themselves. We know the doctrine about a fallen and dangerous world and our purposes here to experience good and evil. We also know that God knows everything and has full power in this world. We know that he prevents some things and allows others. But the explanations specific to our own situations we do not know, or perhaps we do not remember. Nevertheless, we can be satisfied in our spirits over something that our minds cannot explain. We can find the Lord trustworthy even though we do not have all the answers.

As healing sets in, words, especially the Lord's words, can begin to be very helpful. We, the helpers of the sinned-against (or of the broken-hearted sinner), search scripture to select among the Lord's words those that would be most appropriate to help shattered trust mend. These words do not speak so much to the rational mind as they do to the damaged spirit. Priesthood blessings can be very powerful in speaking directly to the offended one's spirit. Through prayer we, the helpers, will find right words, and in due time the Holy Spirit will whisper healing confirmation Spirit to spirit. The Holy Spirit seems to bypass the rational mind and go directly to the damage. So how important it is for all involved to cultivate the Spirit with all their might! Then, as healing proceeds, the urgency for answers to the hows and whys may subside, and the offended one's spirit will begin, if not to understand, at least to accept. He or she may appreciate the meaning behind these words of the Lord: "In all their afflictions he was afflicted. And . . . in his love, and in his pity, he redeemed them, and bore them, and carried them." (D&C 133:53.)

Let us be sure to teach that God always hears our prayers but does not always come when we call him. Let us teach that during the dark hours we can double and triple our faith and our trust until deliverance comes. Let us teach that deliverance will surely come in due time as we turn to him.

Therefore, let us avoid teaching that the gospel will protect us from everything if we are perfect enough and pray hard enough. The gospel is, rather, the resource by which we cope with tribulation and turn our sufferings to good, as Christ did. One woman who suffered abuse agreed with this observation: "One's deepest wounds, integrated, become one's greatest power. It's essential if you want to live a genuine and profound and deep and happy life. It's possible. My life is not exclusive. It's inclusive. And I keep learning." (As quoted in Lois M. Collin, "Actress Reshapes Troubled Past into Life of Love," *Deseret News*, 13 September 1992; see also D&C 112:13.)

We remember that we do not worship God for what he will give us or do for us. We worship God even if he will not deliver us (see Daniel 3:15–18). We worship God because "he doeth not anything save it be for the benefit of the world" (2 Nephi 26:24). We worship him for what he wants to make of us and can make of us, even with all our flaws. Lehi promises his son, Jacob: "In thy childhood thou hast suffered afflictions and much sorrow. . . . Nevertheless . . . thou knowest the greatness of God; and he shall consecrate thine afflictions for thy gain." (2 Nephi 2:1–2.) Finally, we can bear our witness that we know that our lives are in the Lord's hands, and that he will protect us or not, according to his loving plan for each of us.

The sinned-against must ultimately forgive in order for

healing to be completed. But when we teach forgiveness we need to acknowledge that not everything can be quickly forgiven as though it never happened. Forgiveness is a process that must begin with some healing. The grace to forgive is given as the grace to be healed proceeds. Some damage to the sensitive human spirit can be so great that just trying to put it out of one's mind and stuff it down inside is not helpful to the struggling spirit. Here priesthood leaders and loved ones and therapists are needed to help retrain the offended one according to healthy, spiritual principles.

People who have sustained serious abuse have received temporary spiritual damage, although it does not feel temporary. It feels eternal, but it is temporary. All damage innocently incurred will be fully healed—if not in this life, in the life to come. And even that damage which was self-inflicted through sin can be completely healed upon full repentance and faith in the Lord's atonement.

In the case of abuse, the consciousness of the agency that every spirit was created with has been veiled. The protective boundaries have been pulled down and the person who has been sinned against may not know how to put them up again, indeed, may not see any point in trying to set limits anymore. The ability to say no, and mean it, may be gone. A debilitating sense of powerlessness sets in. Therefore, how important it is to teach all our children empowerment through their individual agency. The ability to set our own limits and choose our own path, with heaven's direction, is a tremendously powerful part of spiritual stability. (See 2 Nephi 2:26–27; 10:23; D&C 93:30.)

We used to teach children that they had to do everything an older person, or a person in authority, told them to do. They had to "respect authority." We need to fine-tune our instruction: "Children need to know that adults should not be obeyed in all circumstances just because they are older, a teacher, or even a church leader. Children should be taught that respect—and authority—are things that an individual earns." (In *Confronting Abuse*, ed. Anne L. Horton, B. Kent Harrison, Barry L. Johnson [Salt Lake City: Deseret Book Co., 1993], p. 72.) They need to be taught the sacred principle that liberates women and men from unrighteous dominion, that is, that a person need not be obeyed if he is out of harmony with righteousness.

As a corollary to discerning righteous authority, we need to teach children how to discern and trust the feelings and impressions of the Holy Spirit. This growing ability provides deep feelings of personal security. It is one of the most basic tools that our missionaries teach investigators. The Lord asks us all that we not rely on the arm of flesh but learn to discern divine direction. Our salvation actually depends on it (see D&C 45:57).

Many youth who sit in front of their bishops confessing their sins are locked into sinful behaviors over which they do not have full power. They need help to *become* fully accountable because, (1) they can't always say no when they should, and (2) their sexuality was awakened before their judgment and discipline were. They need help, and many won't get well if left on their own.

How important it is that we teach what constitutes abuse: verbal, emotional, spiritual, or physical (see Mosiah 4:14–15). Let us teach our youth that they are not to abuse others verbally or physically, and let us teach them what to do if someone tries to abuse them.

Perhaps we could teach more about how successful human relationships go forward. Children from troubled families do not understand how to interact in spiritually mature relationships. This ability does not just come naturally—the children have to be taught, and the church is a vital place to teach it. We want to keep singing in Primary "I'm so Glad When Daddy Comes Home," but we may want to temper our idealistic pictures of families with more realism, acknowledging different kinds of families and that all families have their struggles. We might say: "Sometimes things happen in our families that we do not like. Sometimes we can't, by ourselves, make them better. Sometimes maybe we are even hurt." Let us tell children that they can talk to a teacher or to their bishop. Often abused children are very afraid of any authority figure, and speaking to the bishop would be very difficult. But young people can begin to think now of the opportunities they will have in their own families, when they are the parents, to make a good and safe home for their children. The Church can be an important training ground for future families and can help to break the chains of abuse that often pass from generation to generation.

Compassion for sinners needs to underlie all our gospel teaching. We can take for granted that most of our brothers and sisters in the gospel have a deep desire to be clean, pure, and worthy, even though their behavior may appear otherwise. In some this desire is veiled with despair that they will ever be clean.

How then do we teach chastity? That it is a principle of eternal significance cannot be overstated. But let the reader observe the compassion with which President Benson teaches the moral principle: "I recognize that most people fall into sexual sin in a misguided attempt to fulfill basic human needs. We all have a need to feel loved and worthwhile. We all seek to have joy and happiness in our lives. Knowing this, Satan often lures people into immorality by playing on their basic needs. He promises pleasure, happiness, and fulfillment. But this is, of course, a deception." (Ezra Taft Benson, "The Law of Chastity," in *BYU Speeches*, 1987–88, p. 50.)

The prophet teaches that sin is not always just a simple case of being bad, but sometimes of unwisely trying to fill valid needs. A discussion could follow such a statement, asking what kinds of needs a young person might feel that could lead to the misery of immorality. It is our job as leaders and teachers to acknowledge those real needs, and teach that the Lord acknowledges them and has shown how they may be filled for our greatest freedom and happiness.

People are always more important than what they have done. Let all of our images of purity be images showing that purity can be restored: no dead roses that can't be revived, no boards with nail holes in them that cannot be filled, no birds with broken wings who will never fly so high again. I know we have used these things in good faith to try to deter sin, but they are diabolical metaphors because they don't allow for reversal. The Lord's images, on the other hand, reflect miraculous processes because the process of coming clean, of being born again, is miraculous. Take for example, "Though your sins be as scarlet, they shall be as white as snow; though they be red like crimson, they shall be as wool" (Isaiah 1:18; see 1 Corinthians 15:42; Ether 13:9); or, Alma speaking of repentant people, says, "Their garments were washed white through the blood of the Lamb" (Alma 13:11). Yes, sinners have to pay for their sins; yes, blessings will be withheld if they continue in sin; yes, we are plagued with a kind of ritual prodigalism among our youth, but we don't want justice to rob mercy (see Alma 34:15–16).

As I think about Jesus' advocacy of us and our advocacy of each other, I have an impression of the Savior prostrate on the ground in Gethsemane, working out both the pains and anguish of the offended and the sins of the offenders—experiencing these things as though he had been both the offender and the offended. I know that in his heart he despised neither. Rather, his heart was broken in love for the children of men. President Gordon B. Hinckley speaks of Christ's healing power:

> Jesus of Nazareth healed the sick among whom He moved. His regenerating power is with us today to be invoked through His holy priesthood. His divine teachings, his incomparable example, His matchless life, His all-encompassing sacrifice will bring healing to broken hearts, reconciliation to those who argue and shout . . . if sought with humility and forgiveness and love.
>
> As members of the Church of Jesus Christ, ours is a ministry of healing, with a duty to bind the wounds and ease the pain of those who suffer. Upon a world afflicted with greed and contention, upon families distressed by argument and selfishness, upon individuals burdened with sin and troubles and sorrows, I invoke the healing power of Christ, giving my witness of its efficacy and wonder. I testify of Him who is the great source of healing. He is the Son of God, the Redeemer of the world, "The Sun of Righteousness," who came "with healing in his wings." ("The Healing Power of Christ," *Ensign*, November 1988, p. 59.)

CHAPTER THIRTEEN

☙

Filling the Empty Cup

So many things vie for our attention that we can easily lose our sense of what is really important in our search for wholeness. The past wants to hold us prisoner as we obsess over mistakes and other sources of pain. We often feel restless and discontented in the present, and the future holds we know not what, but we fear it does not hold the thing we most want. I want to tell you that there is a particular focus that will bring both a fulness now as well as the future that our hearts long for. The things bothering us most are not outside us—they are inside us, and many of us haven't recognized the true nature of our unhappiness. One problem is that we are not sufficiently acquainted with the *principle of godliness.* We may have esteemed too lightly the bountiful counsel that fills the pages of our scriptures. We may have slipped out of focus spiritually or not yet found that focus.

Joseph Smith observed to the Nauvoo Relief Society on the subject of godliness: "It is one evidence that men are unacquainted with the principle of godliness, to behold the contraction of feeling and lack of charity. The power and glory of godliness [are] spread out on a broad principle to throw out the mantle of charity. God does not look on sin with allowance, but when men have sinned there must be allowance made for them." (*The Words of Joseph Smith*, p. 123.) In the following expression Brigham Young focused even more specifically on that principle: "[We want to teach the saints] to make heaven here by teaching the husband how to live and deal with his wife . . . with his sons and with his daughters; by teaching the wife how to live with and treat her husband and her children, and the husband, wife and children how to live with their neighbors, that all anger and malice and all sin may be overcome by the people and never again gain mastery over them. These are the mysteries that belong to the kingdom of God upon the earth." (*JD* 10:172.)

The truth is that we can't possibly be happy with anger and related sins in our hearts because of our divine origins and because of the unconscious memory of that world we came from. Parley P. Pratt, describing that world, wrote that after God's spirit children were born, they were "matured in the heavenly mansions, trained in the school of love in the family circle, and amid the most tender embraces of parental and fraternal affection" (Parley P. Pratt, *Key to the Science of Theology*, p. 31).

If we are to find wholeness, if we are to begin to establish Zion and prepare for our Savior's return, if we are to inherit the fulness our hearts are longing for, we must plant in our hearts that wholeness is *holiness*. Wholeness and holiness are the condition in which heavenly beings live. If we want to live there with them, we have to practice here and now the manner of emotional and spiritual life that they live. *This* life is the time for men to prepare to meet God (see Alma 34:32). Soon we learn that spirituality and spiritual gifts cannot be separated from loving behavior and feelings. The reason is that both love and spiritual power are attributes of godliness, and neither pure love nor spirituality exists apart from the other.

And it came to pass that there was no contention in the land, because of the love of God which did dwell in the hearts of the people.

And there were no envyings, nor strifes, nor tumults, nor whoredoms, nor lyings, nor murders, nor any manner of lasciviousness; and surely there could not be a happier people among all the people who had been created by the hand of God.

There were no robbers, nor murderers, neither were there Lamanites, nor any manner of -ites; but they were in one, the children of Christ, and heirs to the kingdom of God. And how blessed were they! For the Lord did bless them in all their doings. (4 Nephi 1:15–18.)

The real essence of wholeness, of Zion, of the more excellent way, is taught in D&C 93: "He [the Lord Jesus] received not of the fulness at the first, but received grace for grace; and he received not of the fulness at first, but continued from grace to grace, until he received a fulness; . . . For if you keep my commandments you shall receive of his fulness, and be glorified in me as I am in the Father; therefore, I say unto you, you shall receive grace for grace." (D&C 93:12–13, 20.)

What does this mean: grace for grace and grace to grace? It means that the Lord gave out of his great reservoirs of grace—spiritual gifts his Father had given him—to those around him, and in fact ultimately to the whole human race; in return his Father gave him more gifts of grace. He grew from a portion of divine endowment to a greater endowment and power and glory and love until he was full of grace. Compare Helaman 12:24: "And may God grant, in his great fulness, that men might be brought unto repentance and good works, that they might be restored unto grace for grace, according to their works."

You and I will be restored to grace based on our manifested love of giving grace. The Lord's development is a pattern for you and me. Alma put it this way: "For that which ye do send out shall return unto you again, and be restored" (Alma 41:15). Then what are the gifts of grace that we are to give?

Paul wrote to the Corinthian Saints: "Covet earnestly the best gifts: and yet shew I unto you a more excellent way" (1 Corinthians 12:31).

Then begins Paul's great passage on charity or the pure love of Christ, and how we have to grow up in this gift in Christ. Love is the more excellent way, the most excellent way, because it has the most power to perform miracles in and around the human heart. Charity is a gift of the Holy Ghost. We received the right to charity when hands were laid on our heads for the gift of the Holy Ghost—but only the right, not necessarily the gift until we began to go after it. Mormon wrote: "Wherefore, my beloved brethren, pray unto the Father with all the energy of heart, that ye may be filled with this love, which he hath bestowed upon all who are true followers of his Son, Jesus Christ" (Moroni 7:48).

We may have considered the Holy Ghost an optional gift. We may have been careless about whether we had the gift with us or not. But clearly the gift was given to grow into a constant companion because without obtaining the Spirit as a constant companion we could not prepare to enter Heaven. Brigham Young said to the Saints: "The Elders of Israel, though the great majority of them are moral men, and as clear of spot and blemish as men well can be, live beneath their privilege; they live continually without enjoying the power of God. I want to see men and women breathe the Holy Ghost in every breath of their lives, living constantly in the light of God's countenance." (*JD* 9:288.)

Without cultivating the Holy Ghost as part of the major focus of our lives, we experience the emptiness, the loneliness, of the uncomforted natural man. We are left in our own strength because the nature of the Holy Ghost is that it can't be abundantly bestowed except where one's heart is yearning for it.

But there were times in my life before I knew these truths. During these times, Samuel the Lamanite was speaking to me: "Ye have sought all the days of your lives for that which ye could not obtain; and ye have sought for happiness in doing iniquity, which thing is contrary to the nature of that righteousness which is in our great and Eternal Head" (Helaman 13:38; see also Alma 41:11).

In speaking of the emptiness from which the natural man suffers, we come to the idea of the empty cup. When we feel self-doubt, when we fear our own incapacity or unloveableness, we are tempted to search the faces of those around us for reassurance and love, holding out an empty cup we want them to fill for us. We may have held out the cup in the past and someone, full of grace, put something in it we needed so much at the time. The problem with the empty cup is that holding it out can become a habit, a way of life—we look to others for that which they cannot provide because in looking to them continually we are violating the principle of grace for grace. The Lord has so designed it that we find the answers and the fulness we need while we are putting grace into someone else's cup.

We can see how it is a powerful act of faith to give when we feel empty; it is the reaching into Elijah's cornmeal barrel during a famine and coming up full (see 1 Kings 17:16). But the return is always greater than if we had sought directly. Of course we are not giving so that someone else will give—that would not be pure love; we are giving because holiness is wholeness, because it is the more excellent way.

Sometimes we find ourselves holding the cup out for something other than reassurance. We hold out the cup in expectation that those around us will put in what we want them to do or to be. We criticize our poor husbands who have a hard time measuring up to our expectations, our children, our neighbors, because they do not put in the cup what we think they should. We think or say, "Can't they see I'm right?" and we withdraw our grace from them. We feel discontented, but we think those around us are the cause of our discontent. How easily we live in pointless conflict generated by pride and by ignorance of the wiles of the devil, rending precious relationships. The way to peace is simple. In my own life I found out that the empty cup syndrome doesn't work because it is a violation of the grace-for-grace principle of godliness.

We tend to see life's experiences as random, helter-skelter, in their design, but it would appear that all the people in our lives are there for important reasons. We stand in a sacred relationship to them. They and we cannot be made perfect without each other. By divine design, they are not there to satisfy us. Rather, they are given to us to make possible a much greater love than we would have been capable of in a situation where everybody agreed with us, everybody loved us, everybody saw everything the way we do. They are there to change us and to tell us what we need to know and to help us evolve along godly lines. Those who are difficult and abrasive in our lives are friends in disguise. They are there to teach us to perfect love in ourselves, not to perfect them.*

Because we are godly beings in our most basic nature, we cannot act in ungodly ways without being unhappy. When godliness is understood and embraced, one has happiness. Alma taught that those who have gone contrary to the nature of God are in a state contrary to the nature of happiness (see Alma 41:11). These are eternal principles, and they are true now and forever. How could it be any other way? I have been in that state contrary to the nature of God many times, not so much from deliberate rebellion as from having been ignorant of or having esteemed lightly the plain counsel abounding in the scriptures.

Here are two things that have made a big difference in my life:

1. I needed to learn to discern between negative energy and positive energy. I needed to learn that Satan is behind the discontented, bad mood and that he knows more about the powers of godliness than we do and how to scramble divine things. Our disdain, our brittleness with others, our impatience, our intolerance—these are evil.

We may feel that our bad dispositions and abusive behavior rule us, that we can't rule them, but that is Satan's message. The truth is that by the use of our powerful agency we can and

---

*I am speaking of typical daily abrasions, not of relationships where women may be abused. Those are to be escaped from.

do generate any kind of energy we choose. We are not victims of Satan unless we fail to discern him. To give us power over Satan was one of the main reasons why priesthood hands were laid on our heads to give us the Holy Ghost. Brigham Young said in connection with the subtle works of Satan: "There are thousands of plans which the enemy of all righteousness employs to decoy the hearts of the people away from righteousness" (*JD* 3:194). Joseph Smith focused the idea to relationships: "The policy of the wicked spirit is to separate what God has joined together, and unite what He [God] has separated, which the devil has succeeded in doing to admiration in the present state of society" (*TPJS*, p. 103). The Apostle Paul wrote: "Put on the whole armour of God, that ye may be able to stand against the wiles of the devil. For we wrestle not against flesh and blood, but against principalities, against powers, against the rulers of the darkness of this world." (Ephesians 6:11–12.)

Satan seeks to rend the Saints' relationships so that Zion cannot be established. We forget in the very moment we ought not that Satan and his followers promote contention (see 3 Nephi 11:29) by stirring around in the pride in the Saints' hearts. King Benjamin said, "But, O my people, beware lest there shall arise contentions among you, and ye list to obey the evil spirit" (Mosiah 2:32). Brigham Young asked:

> Do we know how to rise in the morning? Do we leave our couches in the morning with anger in our hearts? Do we feel disconsolate, afflicted and oppressed by the Adversary? We can get rid of all this by going down upon our knees and praying until we overcome that feeling of discontent and misery and become kind to our companions and offspring, to the inmates of our habitation, to our flocks and herds, to our neighbors and to every creature God has made. . . . Get down upon our knees and pray until we are filled with the Spirit of peace. I may say, my wife is hurrying me and I feel out of sorts; perhaps I have not had very pleasant dreams, have thought somebody was abusing me or got angry with somebody in my sleep, and I rise in the morning tired and feeling unpleasant with myself and

everybody around me: while the Elder who has dreamed of preaching the Gospel to the nations, of building up Zion and laboring for the Gospel all night in his mind and feelings, being filled with the Holy Ghost, rejoices in his sleep; his slumbers are sweet to him and he rises in the morning filled with the good Spirit, and with him it is, "God bless you, wife, God bless you my children. . . .

We are in one of the strongholds of Zion; let us, therefore, so live that our days and nights will be pleasant unto us, and never spend an hour without the light of truth beaming upon our understandings. (*JD* 10:173–174.)

To choose positive, affirming, tolerant, forgiving, Spirit-filled energy over negative energy is to choose godliness over evil. I think it's that simple. There are finally only two forces at work on us, and they are continually at work; and until we learn to discern and reject most negative energy, we will be victimized by it.

What we may not have realized is that our positive energy is, when pure and free, continuous with the Spirit of the Lord. There are, in fact, emotional states which either attract or repel the Spirit of the Lord. Encouragement, loving tolerance, forgiveness, gratitude, reinforcing the good, reverence for others, love for God and his creations, faith that things are going right for our particular needs at this particular time, assurance that there is a benevolent, orchestrating hand in our lives—all these are states of rest and godliness and they are within our power in any moment. They are the states out of which deeper and deeper levels of healing love develop. When we use our agency to generate these positive energies, the Holy Ghost, who is always at the ready, always seeking access (see Alma 5:37–38)—who never slumbers or sleeps—is drawn to us and enlarges on what we are doing. These ways of acting and feeling and thinking draw him, and he comes with his divine gifts to heal and sanctify us. Since the Holy Ghost was not given as an optional power, we want to do all in our power to cultivate this Spirit every waking moment of our lives. That is done by taking thought to invite him and paying attention to the people around us in reverent ways.

One particular thing I am becoming aware of is that there is some kind of connection that wants to be made between my spirit and the spirits of the people around me and the Lord. I do not understand it entirely yet. But what if life were entirely fabricated to teach us the lessons we need to know, even down to the people crossing our paths day in and day out and even to the things these people have to say to us? King Benjamin said, "Open your ears that ye may hear, and your hearts that ye may understand, and your minds that the mysteries of God may be unfolded to your view" (Mosiah 2:9). What if our only real assignment in life was to listen carefully, with reverence, being touched in an intimate way, changing and evolving from our associations with each other, listening to the people trying to get our attention and to give us messages, consciously or unconsciously?

I am learning that being task-oriented, being too attached to my day-planner, misses the point of life: tasks are just means by which God gets us together so that we can affirm and encourage and bless and learn from each other. It is people-work that really matters. People are not interruptions in what we want to get done—they are the reason we're here! The people who bother and annoy us probably have a message we don't want to hear.

I want to discuss the face for a moment, remembering that the Lord Jesus Christ is our model. Mormon describes that luminous incident between the resurrected Savior and the Nephites: "And it came to pass that Jesus blessed them as they did pray unto him; and his countenance did smile upon them, and the light of his countenance did shine upon them, and behold they were as white as the countenance and also the garments of Jesus. . . . And behold, they did pray steadfastly, without ceasing, unto him; and he did smile upon them again; and behold they were white, even as Jesus." (3 Nephi 19:25, 30.) Jesus was communicating the Spirit to his disciples by turning his face to them and by smiling at them. Spirit was coming from his smiling face and entering into their souls and purifying them (see 3 Nephi 19:28).

The Spirit is also communicated through our eyes and our

smile. We cannot underestimate the healing power that our loving expressions and our warm smiles can impart. We do not really even need to speak. In and of themselves, smiles and loving light in the eyes have their own healing power. They enter the non-verbal receptors of those who receive them and do small miracles to their souls. Many have spoken of looking into the eyes of a prophet, or being smiled on by him, and feeling as though they had received a blessing. They had. How did those prophets get that power? By enlarging on what they already possessed in its rudimentary spiritual form. You are familiar with this benediction from Numbers 6:24–26:

"The Lord bless thee, and keep thee:

"The Lord make his face shine upon thee, and be gracious unto thee:

"The Lord lift up his countenance upon thee, and give thee peace."

What if God were seeking to organize our time so that we could give grace to others? Having realized that, I would learn to live in the present moment making a connection with that delicate Spirit through trying to hear the spirits of the people around me. I believe that this is moving me forward to greater wholeness. What is the connection between my ability to hear the word of the Lord and my ability to give my full attention, without letting my mind wander, to those around me? I wonder if I listen to the Lord about as well as I listen to other people.

So what shall we put in each other's cups? Positive energy consisting of affirmations of the other person, appreciation, forgiveness, strength, deep listening, a willingness to change what needs changing, and to maintain this delicate connection that's trying to establish itself between my spirit and the spirits of those around me and with the Lord. I want to remember not to set out in any situation with an empty cup, but to carry a treasure of delicate spiritual gifts to put in the cups of my brothers and sisters. "Strengthen your brethren in all your conversation, in all your prayers, in all your exhortations, and in all your doings" (D&C 108:7). In this way we find the fulness our hearts long for. We find a very reason to live!

Index